archiving websites

a practical guide for information management professionals

archiving websites
a practical guide for information management professionals

Adrian Brown

facet publishing

© Adrian Brown 2006

Published by
Facet Publishing
7 Ridgmount Street
London WC1E 7AE
www.facetpublishing.co.uk

Facet Publishing is wholly owned by CILIP: the Chartered Institute of Library and Information Professionals.

First published 2006

British Library Cataloguing in Publication Data
A catalogue record for this book is available from the British Library.

ISBN-13: 978-1-85604-553-7
ISBN-10: 1-85604-553-6

Typeset in 11/15 pt University Old Style and Zurich Expanded by Facet Publishing.
Printed and made in Great Britain by MPG Books Ltd, Bodmin, Cornwall.

Contents

Acknowledgements

This book would not have been possible without the innovative research and expertise of a number of individuals and organizations working in the field of web archiving around the world. In particular, I was privileged to be invited to speak at the 'Archiving Web Resources' international conference hosted by the National Library of Australia in Canberra, November 2004. The opportunity to hear about and discuss the experiences and ideas of so many colleagues over a number of years, but especially at this unique event, has been an unparalleled source of inspiration.

I must also acknowledge my considerable debt to colleagues at The National Archives, the Internet Archive, the European Archive and in the UK Web Archiving Consortium, working with whom has provided the basis for so much of this book. I would particularly like to express my gratitude to the friends and colleagues who have read, and provided so much valuable comment on, drafts of this book: Ian Hodges, David Thomas and Malcolm Todd of The National Archives, and Claire Jones of English Heritage. Their generosity and expertise has enriched this book immeasurably and, of course, any errors or omissions remain the sole responsibility of the author.

I would like to thank all those individuals and organizations who have given permission to reproduce illustrations and other material: Figures 1.1, 1.2, 4.1 and 4.2 (Crown Copyright), 2.1, 4.3 and 7.7 (National Library of Australia), 2.2 (Library of Congress), 6.6, 7.3, 7.4 and 9.2 (The National Archives), 7.1 and 7.2 (State Library of Tasmania), 7.5 and 7.6 (National Library of Norway) and 9.1 and Appendix 2 (UK Web Archiving Consortium). Crown Copyright material is reproduced with the permission of the Controller of HMSO and the Queen's Printer for Scotland.

This book is dedicated to my friends and family, for the support which made it possible, and in particular to Sally, for keeping me and everything else going while I was writing it, to Ruth and Leno, for their own new edition, and to my Dad, who would have been proud.

Adrian Brown

Glossary

Bit: The fundamental unit of digital information storage, which can represent a binary value of either 1 or 0.

Blog: A contraction of 'weblog', a blog is a form of online journal, typically authored by an individual and updated on a frequent basis.

Byte: A unit of measurement of data volume, normally equivalent to 8 bits.

Checksum: A form of error detection which calculates a value based on the content of a piece of information. This value can then be used to compare different copies of the same piece of information. More complex forms of checksum include cyclic redundancy checks and cryptographic hash functions, such as MD5 and SHA-1.

Cookie: A piece of information sent by a web server to a web browser, which is stored on the user's computer and sent back to the server every time it is accessed by that browser. Cookies are typically used to identify or authenticate users, principally to track access or allow personalization of web pages.

DNS: See domain name system.

Domain: The host web server of a website, distinguished by a unique domain name.

Domain name: The unique name of a web server. In a URL, the domain name immediately follows the network communications protocol scheme identifier (e.g. 'www.mysite.com' in 'www.mysite.com/about/about_mysite.html').

Domain name system: The distributed global system which maintains information about the domain names that comprise a network such as the internet. The DNS records the IP address associated with each domain name. This, for example, allows an HTTP request for a URL from a web browser to be routed to the correct physical web server.

Exabyte: A unit of measurement of data volume, equivalent to 1000 petabytes.

File transfer protocol: A type of network communications protocol used for transferring files over the internet.

FTP: See file transfer protocol.

Gigabyte: A unit of measurement of data volume, equivalent to 1000 megabytes.

HTTP: See hypertext transfer protocol.

Hypertext transfer protocol: A type of network communications protocol used to convey requests and responses between web clients (such as web browsers) and web servers.

Internet protocol address: The unique number used to designate every device which is connected to a network. Principally used on the internet, it allows communications to be correctly routed between devices, such as web servers and web clients.

IP address: See internet protocol address.

JavaScript: An object-oriented scripting language, commonly used to add functionality to web pages.

Kilobyte: A unit of measurement of data volume, equivalent to 1000 bytes.

Megabyte: A unit of measurement of data volume, equivalent to 1000 kilobytes.

Oersted: The unit of measurement for magnetic field intensity.

Path: The name which indicates the location of a computer file within a file system. In the context of the web, the path is the part of a URL which follows the domain name, and indicates the location of a file on the host web server (e.g. about/about_mysite.html in www.mysite.com/about/about_mysite.html).

Petabyte: A unit of measurement of data volume, equivalent to 1000 terabytes.

Really simple syndication: An XML format for syndicating web content – that is, making that content automatically available for use in other websites. Common uses include newsfeeds and blogs.

Robot exclusion notice: A convention to control which parts of a website are accessible to web crawling software, comprising a set of rules specified in a 'robots.txt' file located in the top-level directory of a website.

RSS: See really simple syndication.

SQL: See structured query language.

Structured query language: A language for creating, modifying and retrieving data from relational database systems. It is defined as an ISO standard (ISO 9075-1-14: 2003), although many variants are found among relational database management systems.

Terabyte: A unit of measurement of data volume, equivalent to 1000 gigabytes.

Uniform resource identifier: A protocol for identifying networked resources, such as web content.

Uniform resource locator: A type of URI which identifies both the resource and its location. It therefore acts as an address for networked resources such as web content.

URI: See uniform resource identifier.

URL: See uniform resource locator.

User agent: A client-side computer program which uses a particular network protocol. The most common type of user agent is a web browser.

Web browser: A computer program which enables a user to view and navigate web content. Specifically, a browser is an HTTP client, capable of submitting HTTP requests to a web server and interpreting the responses.

Web crawler: A computer program which automatically browses web pages, retrieving the content and recursively following the links contained therein, according to predefined parameters. Web crawlers are typically used by search engines, to build their search indexes, and for web archiving.

Web server: A computer program which receives HTTP requests from clients (usually web browsers), and 'serves' the requested web content to them. The term may also be applied to the computer on which the web server software is running.

Wiki: A form of collaborative website, whereby users can easily add and update content online.

XML: Extensible Markup Language: a general-purpose markup language, designed for creating special purpose markup languages to describe many different kinds of data. It is intended to facilitate data exchange, particularly across the internet.

Chapter 1

Introduction

The world wide web is such a pervasive cultural phenomenon that it is easy to forget its relative infancy. Although the internet itself can trace its origins to ARPANET, the computer network developed by the US military in the late 1960s, the world wide web has a much more recent history. Its birth can, arguably, be assigned a very precise date: at 2:56:20 pm on 6 August 1991, the world's first website was made available on the public internet by Tim Berners-Lee at CERN, the European Organization for Nuclear Research.[1] The privatization of the internet's backbone infrastructure in 1995 opened the door to commercialization, and its original academic and scientific usage was rapidly subsumed as public and commercial interest escalated. To describe its expansion, from that prototype system for information exchange within the high-energy physics community to the global information network of today, as dramatic is an understatement. By 2005, the public web was estimated to comprise over 11.5 billion web pages.[2] And the public part of the web is the minority: the so-called 'deep web' – content which is inaccessible to search engines or to which access is controlled – is thought to be 500 times larger.[3]

The technological development of the web has been equally remarkable. This can be illustrated graphically with examples of government websites taken from the collections of The National Archives of the UK. Figure 1.1

shows the home page of the Home Office website in 2000, and Figure 1.2 is taken from the same site in 2005.

Figure 1.1　　UK Home Office website in 2000 (Crown Copyright)

Figure 1.2　　UK Home Office website in 2005 (Crown Copyright)

The 2000 website, typically for its era, was primarily text-based, with only rudimentary graphical and design elements. Only five years later, the same site offers sophisticated graphics, intelligent searching, audio, video and animated content, and live news feeds. It is instructive and perhaps a little alarming to see how the technologies which, at the time, seemed exciting and innovative can, in such a brief period, come to appear so primitive.

During the course of this extraordinary growth, the web has evolved into perhaps the single most dominant communication channel in the world. The 'Google generation' not only search for information on the web, they also use it to shop, bank, watch television, chat to friends and family, book their holidays and play games. They expect to be able to access an ever-increasing range of services online, from checking train timetables to paying their taxes.

Equally, providers of information and services have been quick to adopt the web, and increasingly do so to the exclusion of more traditional methods. The growth of e-journals, either as electronic counterparts to paper publications or as exclusively online publications, is just one example of this trend. Although the drive to provide an ever-greater array of online services may sometimes misjudge the demand, as demonstrated by the 'dotcom' boom and bust of the late 1990s and early 2000s, there can be no doubting the general trend.

However, scale and ubiquity are not the only noteworthy characteristics of the world wide web: transience is another of its defining properties. In a 2001 study, it was estimated that the average lifespan of a web page is between 75 and 100 days.[4] In an online world where anyone can instantly publish via personal blogs, and information consumers prize immediacy of access over provenance, the emphasis is very much on information publication rather than retention. Indeed, the ease with which content can be made available via the web, combined with the fragility of that content in a world of constant technological change, engenders an information environment which can be positively hostile to long-term sustainability.

It is therefore not surprising that the emergence of the world wide web has been accompanied by concerns about the preservation of its content. Libraries, archives and other cultural organizations, together with government bodies, higher and further education institutions and the commercial sector, all have potential interests in ensuring that information is preserved and maintained with a greater degree of certainty than if it were simply left to the vagaries of the online world. Libraries must reflect the increasing move towards online publication; archives need to adapt to the world of e-government and e-business, where records are created and disseminated electronically and citizens interact with the state via a web browser; and commercial organizations must understand both the value of information assets and the legal implications of doing business on the web.

A wide range of organizations is therefore increasingly identifying the need to collect and preserve specific elements of the web, from national domains or individual subject areas to an organization's own website. Web archiving is not just the province of large national institutions – smaller organizations, such as local archives and museums, learned societies and publishers, are also beginning to consider their roles. There is now a growing wealth of international experience in the field of web archiving, marked by the establishment of the first public web archives in a number of different countries. However, most research has so far taken place in relative isolation and been of a highly technical nature, offering little or no practical guidance to information management professionals seeking to implement programmes of their own. The substantial body of information extant on the technical aspects of web archiving is primarily aimed at an audience of already active practitioners.

This book seeks to redress this issue, having been written with the intention of providing a broader introduction and overview, specifically for those who may be considering taking their first steps into the world of web archiving, or who may simply wish to gain an understanding of the issues. It is intended to reflect the needs and concerns of those with an interest in web archiving at all scales, not merely those in large cultural institutions – smaller organizations also have a potentially very important role to play, either individually or as part of consortia. Although it is impossible to write about a subject such as web archiving without touching upon technical issues, this book deliberately avoids their detailed consideration. References to sources of further information are provided for those who wish to delve more deeply into such matters and, in particular, Appendix 1 provides information about specific software tools mentioned in the text. However, it is considered that those with managerial or curatorial responsibility, who wish to understand the issues and processes more than the technology, suffer from the greater dearth of information. Furthermore, by taking this approach it is hoped that this book will be rather less at the mercy of technological change, and its useful life accordingly greater.

This book provides an overview of current best practice, together with practical guidance for anyone seeking to establish a web archiving programme. It is intended to be of value to both technical and non-technical readers, and especially to meet the needs of three audiences:

- policy makers, who need to make decisions about establishing or developing an institutional web archiving programme: Chapters 8 and 9 provide an overview of the benefits, risks, resource implications and other management issues
- information management professionals, who may be required to implement a web archiving programme: Chapters 3–7 offer detailed guidance on principles and practice, illustrated by, but not limited to, current technological approaches
- website owners and webmasters, who may be required to facilitate archiving of their own websites: in particular, Chapter 4 includes an insight into the impact of archiving requirements on website design and management.

The web archiving process can viewed as a workflow, whereby web resources are selected, collected, preserved, and delivered to users. This is illustrated in Figure 1.3 (overleaf); the model is described in more detail in subsequent chapters.

The first chapter provides a rapid survey of the history of web archiving, up to and including current initiatives. The following chapters consider the various stages of the web archiving process, from the initial selection of content, through methods of collection, quality assurance, cataloguing and long-term preservation, to the delivery of archived material to end users. The complex legal implications of web archiving are also considered. The penultimate chapter examines the broader question of establishing

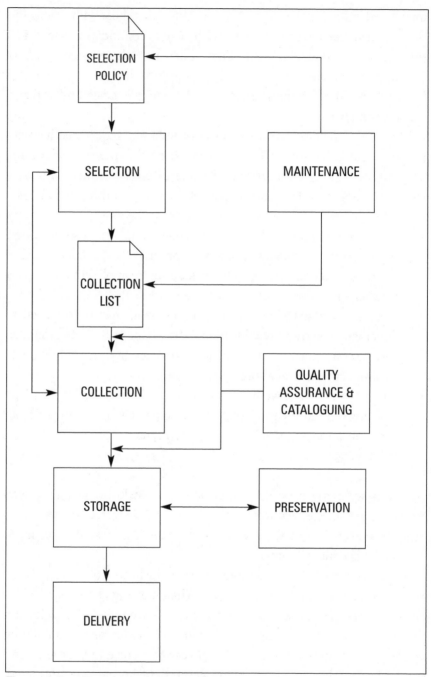

Figure 1.3   The web archiving process

and managing a web archiving programme, considering the available options and the organizational implications. The final chapter looks to the future, examining emerging trends and their potential impacts.

Notes and references

1 See www.time.com/time/80days/910806 [accessed 18 February 2006]. The first web server at CERN (http://info.cern.ch/) became operational in late 1990, but the cited date marks the moment when that web server became publicly available across the internet.

2 See www.cs.uiowa.edu/~asignori/web-size/ [accessed 18 February 2006].

3 Bergman. M. K. (2001) The Deep Web: surfacing hidden value, *Journal of Electronic Publishing,* **7** (1), www.press.umich.edu/ep/07-01/ bergman.html [accessed 23 November 2004].

4 This estimate was made in a study by Alexa Internet, cited in Day (2003, 7). See Day, M. (2003) *Collecting and Preserving the World Wide Web: a feasibility study undertaken for the JISC and Wellcome Trust,* JISC and Wellcome Trust, http://library.welcome.ac.uk/assets/wt/039229.pdf [accessed 23 October 2005].

Chapter 2

The development of web archiving

Introduction

The history of web archiving is almost as long as that of the web itself. There are grounds for optimism in noting that, in a world where modern technological innovations, such as the first e-mail, have all too often been lost forever, the very first website is still preserved: that initial page of text and hyperlinks created in 1991 (see Chapter 1, Introduction) can still be viewed and navigated today.[1] The first notable web archiving initiative was also, and remains to this day, the most ambitious. The Internet Archive was established in 1996, with the mission statement of 'universal access to all human knowledge'.[2] Since then, web archiving has rapidly evolved to become an international, multidisciplinary concern, spawning a multitude of research- and practically based programmes. This chapter describes some of the major milestones along that road, from the very first web archiving initiatives to the latest international research.

Initiation: the Internet Archive

The origins of the Internet Archive lie in Alexa Internet, a web cataloguing company founded by Brewster Kahle and Bruce Gilliat in 1996. At the same time, Kahle established the Internet Archive as a non-profit organization, with the aim of building a digital library to offer permanent access to historical collections which exist in digital form. Alexa harvests a snapshot of the world wide web every two months, each snapshot encompassing over 35 million websites.[3] These snapshots are donated to the Internet Archive, and form the basis of its main collection.

Located in San Francisco, the Internet Archive is undoubtedly the largest web archive in the world. The raw statistics make impressive reading: as of 2005, the archive contained over 40 billion web pages; the total collection amounted to over one petabyte (1000 terabytes) of data, and was increasing at a rate of 20 terabytes per month.

The Internet Archive collects material by remote harvesting, the method used by the vast majority of web archiving programmes at present. This uses specialized web crawling software to copy web resources remotely, and is described in more detail in Chapter 4, Collection Methods. To date, these harvests have been collected using Alexa Internet's own, proprietary web crawling software, which is not available for direct use by the Internet Archive or other organizations. In order to perform its own harvesting, and develop improved crawling techniques, the Internet Archive began development of Heritrix, its own open-source archival quality crawler. Increasingly used by the Archive for its own collecting, Heritrix now also forms the basis for development of the International Internet Preservation Consortium (IIPC) web crawler (see later in this chapter). The results of each crawl are stored in the ARC data format, developed by Alexa Internet and the Internet Archive specifically for this purpose. The ARC format forms the basis of subsequent work by the IIPC to develop a standard web archiving format (see later in this chapter).

Faced with the problem of how to store very large volumes of data cheaply and make that data immediately available to online users, the Archive developed a solution based on clusters of low-cost, low-power, modified off-the-shelf PCs, which combine to provide an extensible architecture for very high volumes of data. The Archive's increasing storage demands led it to commercialize the technology in the shape of the Petabox, a disk-based storage solution which is scalable to one petabyte.[4]

Access to the collection is provided by the Wayback Machine, an innovative time-based index and interface which not only provides access to individual website snapshots, but also allows them to be browsed within their historical context. Although currently proprietary, the Internet Archive is developing an open-source version of the software.[5] The Wayback Machine is described in more detail in Chapter 7, Delivery to Users.

Given the scale of its collecting, it would be impractical for the Internet Archive to seek the explicit permission of every website owner to harvest their content. The Archive therefore operates an 'opt-out' policy, whereby it will remove any material from the collection at the request of the owner. It also offers detailed instructions to webmasters on how to limit the harvesting or completely exclude their web content from being harvested. However, the Archive's approach to copyright legislation does create potentially serious difficulties, not least exposing the Archive to the possibility of litigation, explored in more detail in Chapter 8, Legal Issues.

In late 1999, the Archive increased its scope to begin collecting a much wider range of materials, including digitized books, audio material such as recordings of live concerts, television and film material, and obsolete, freeware or shareware software. In 2003, the Internet Archive donated a copy of its web archive to the Bibliotheca Alexandrina, the 'New Library of Alexandria' in Egypt, which is maintained as a duplicate of the US collection.[6] This is part of a broader plan to create mirror collections in Europe, Asia and Africa, in order to increase availability and contribute to the long-term sustainability of the archive. The second of these centres to be established is the European Digital Archive, described later in this chapter.

The Internet Archive continues to play a major role in the continued development of web archiving technologies. It is a major partner in the IIPC, and its innovative tools form the basis for much of the IIPC's work to create an open, standard web archiving toolkit. The work of the IIPC is described later in this chapter.

Diversification: the spread of web archiving

Since the emergence of the Internet Archive, a number of international, national and institutional web archiving programmes have been established. Although space and practicality do not permit an exhaustive description of every such programme, the following selective examples do offer some indication of the variety of scale and approach.

Web archiving in the Nordic countries: the Nordic Web Archive and associated projects

Web archiving has a comparatively long history in the Nordic countries, and is notable for a tradition of practical application and innovative tool development.

The National Library of Sweden's Kulturarw3 project, which began in 1996, ranks among the longest-running web archiving programmes. It undertakes large-scale, periodic harvesting of the entire Swedish web domain. The project collects websites by remote harvesting, using the Combine harvesting program developed in 1998 by NetLab at Lund University.[7] By the beginning of 2005, the project had collected nearly 350,000 websites from the Swedish domain, amounting to some 10 terabytes of data, and counting as one of the largest web archives in the world. The collection is hosted by the Library, which also provides passive preservation facilities. The collection is only available to on-site users.

The Nordic Web Archive (NWA) was a collaborative initiative between the national libraries of Denmark, Finland, Iceland, Norway and Sweden. It was established in 1997 to co-ordinate and share experience between the various national projects. It also specifically aimed to develop tools and methods for web archiving, and its most significant contribution in this area was the development of the NWA Toolset, an open-source access and delivery system for large web archives, released in 2004. The NWA partners were instrumental in the formation of the International Internet Preservation Coalition (see later in this chapter) and, since 2003, the development focus has shifted to WERA (WEb ARchive Access),[8] an access system which is based on, and replaces, the NWA Toolset, and is being developed as part of the IIPC Toolkit.

As participants in the EU-funded NEDLIB project (see below), the Finnish and Norwegian National Libraries contributed to the development of the NEDLIB Harvester, which has subsequently been used in a number of web archiving programmes, perhaps the most notable being several large-scale harvests of the Finnish web domain since 2000. Finland's EVA programme, which has its origins in pilot projects begun in 1997, has adopted a similar approach to the Swedish Kulturarw3 programme, collecting regular snapshots across the national domain.

The Royal Library of Denmark has been undertaking selective collection, as part of legal deposit legislation, since 1998. In 2002 the Royal Library, with the State and University Library at Aarhus, began a pilot project called Netarchive.dk, to develop a strategy for archiving Danish internet material.[9] At the conclusion of this project in 2004, a collaborative approach had been developed whereby the Royal Library would take regular snapshots of the Danish web domain, while the State and University Library would concentrate on selective and thematic collection. In both cases, remote harvesting is the preferred collection method.

The National Library of Norway's Paradigma project,[10] which commenced in 2001, was designed to meet the requirements of legal deposit for digital publications. Large-scale remote harvests of the Norwegian web domain took place in 2002–3, and the Library also takes daily snapshots of 65 online newspapers.

Pandora

The National Library of Australia (NLA) established its Pandora (Preserving and Accessing Networked Documentary Resources of Australia) programme in 1996, and it can therefore be counted among the first web archives to be developed.[11] Pandora was originally envisaged as a collaborative venture, allowing state libraries and other Australian cultural collecting agencies to share facilities. Ten partners currently contribute to Pandora.

Pandora collects online publications, which may equate to entire websites or to particular website content. It adopts a highly selective approach, and its collecting policy encompasses publications which are by Australian authors, or are about Australia. The collecting policies of the partners are complementary: for example, NLA and the state libraries collect material of national and state significance, respectively. Each partner identifies and collects material of interest within its own collecting policy, and the permission of every publisher is sought before collection.

Material is collected by remote harvesting, initially using a variety of freely available web crawling tools, but latterly using NLA's own PANDAS (Pandora Digital Archiving System) software.[12] Developed in 2001, PANDAS has been designed to support the archiving workflows of the Pandora partners. These include:

- identification, selection and registration of titles
- management of the permissions process
- configuring and executing harvesting
- quality assurance
- cataloguing
- assignment of persistent identifiers in accordance with the NLA's scheme[13]
- online delivery to users.

PANDAS currently uses HTTrack as its default crawler, although in principle other crawlers can also be plugged in. NLA has continued to develop PANDAS, with new versions released in 2003 and planned for 2005/6. However, in the longer term PANDAS may be replaced by the tools being developed by the IIPC (see later in this chapter).

The collection currently includes nearly 20,000 snapshots of 10,000 distinct websites. All sites are freely available online (see Figure 2.1 overleaf), and long-term preservation of the collection will be provided by NLA, as it develops its in-house facilities.

HTTrack and other web crawlers

Although not designed specifically to support web archiving, the widespread availability of web crawler software has been a major factor in the ability of so many organizations to begin web archiving programmes. The most widely used tool in this context is HTTrack, a free, open-source web crawler developed by Xavier Roche.[14] Appearing under numerous guises, including 'offline browsers' and 'website copiers', there are countless tools available to copy online content automatically, including Mercator, developed by Compaq's Systems Research Centre and subsequently used in the AltaVista search engine,[15] and Teleport Pro, a commercial product.

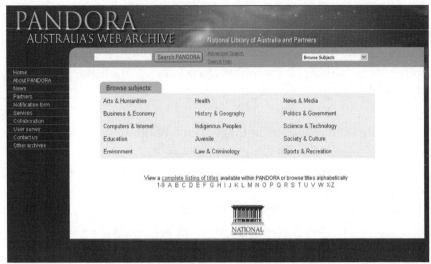

Figure 2.1   Pandora (National Library of Australia)

These tools may be available as freeware, shareware and fully commercial products. However, in the vast majority of cases, their applicability to web archiving, at least for anything beyond single websites, is very limited. The recent development of crawlers designed specifically for web archiving, such as Heritrix (see below), is beginning to render their use obsolete.

NEDLIB

In 1997, the European Commission funded a project to develop methods for harvesting web material to support legal deposit in European libraries. The NEDLIB (Networked European Deposit Library) project was led by the Koninklijke Bibliotheek (the National Library of the Netherlands), with multiple partners, including eight national libraries and one national archive.[16] After testing a variety of existing web crawlers, including Combine, the project developed its own. Released in 2000, the NEDLIB Harvester was one of the first web crawlers to be specifically designed for archival purposes. It has subsequently been used in a number of web archiving programmes, including trial harvesting of the Dutch, Estonian and Icelandic web domains, and a crawl of the Lithuanian webspace in 2002 by the Martynas Mažvydas National Library of Lithuania. Although still available, the NEDLIB Harvester is due to be widely replaced by the Heritrix tool.

Bibliothèque nationale de France

The Bibliothèque nationale de France (BnF) has been developing and testing a range of innovative web archiving techniques since 2000.[17] Its overall strategy combines a number of different approaches to selection, including periodic crawls of the entire French web domain, thematic collections, archiving of selected deep web sites and continuous crawling of automatically selected sites. To achieve all this, the BnF has undertaken two pilot projects: the first tested methods for automatically identifying and harvesting sites, using link ranking, and the second investigated techniques to capture database-driven sites, leading to the development of the DeepArc tool described later in this chapter. Both types of approach are discussed in more detail in Chapter 4, Collection Methods. The BnF has conducted a large-scale crawl of the French webspace, and a focused crawl of sites relating to the elections in 2002.

MINERVA

MINERVA (Mapping the Internet Electronic Resources Virtual Archive) is the Library of Congress's web archiving project (Figure 2.2).[18] Beginning with a pilot project in 2000, MINERVA now provides the Library with the capability to conduct selective web archiving on a significant scale: by 2004, the Library had captured over 36,000 websites.

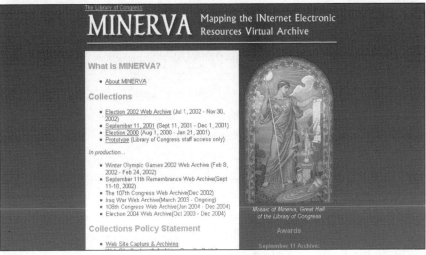

Figure 2.2   MINERVA (Library of Congress)

Although the Library's collecting policy does allow for the selection of individual websites that meet its selection criteria, to date it has largely adopted a subject-based, thematic collecting policy. Events which are deemed to be of historical interest, and which are reflected within the web domain, are identified. The collection of sites relating to those events is then managed as a project: funding and partners are secured, the collection list is agreed, permissions are sought and the material is collected and ingested into the collection. Current collections cover the 2000 presidential election, the events of 9/11 and the 2002 elections. Collections in preparation include the 2002 Winter Olympics, the Iraq War and the 2004 election.

Sites are collected by remote harvesting, and the Library works with a variety of partners on the collection process. For example, the Internet Archive has been contracted to harvest the websites, and to provide the Wayback Machine software to manage and provide access to the collection, and WebArchivist.org has helped to develop new methods of identifying, cataloguing and presenting websites. The Library itself hosts the various collections, some of which are accessible online whereas others can only be accessed on-site at the Library. It is anticipated that long-term preservation facilities for the collection will be developed as part of the National Digital Information Infrastructure and Preservation (NDIIP) programme (see Chapter 10, Future Trends).

DACHS

The Digital Archive of Chinese Studies (DACHS) project was established in 2001 to identify, archive and make accessible social and cultural web resources of relevance to Chinese studies.[19] It has a particular focus on social and political material in the Chinese web domain. This project is jointly managed by the Institute of Chinese Studies at the University of Heidelberg and the Sinological Institute at Leiden University, and is an excellent example of a relatively small-scale, focused and highly successful web archive. DACHS uses a selective approach, with material being primarily collected by remote harvesting, together with some voluntary donations. As a consequence of its collection policy, DACHS is particularly notable for its archiving of discussion lists.

WARP

The National Diet Library in Japan began its Web Archiving Programme (WARP) in 2002, in response to changes in legal deposit legislation.[20] The WARP programme includes both snapshots of Japanese websites and selective collection of e-journals. WARP collects material through a combination of direct transfer and remote harvesting. As of 2004, 600 websites and 1,100 journals had been collected. The Library is currently investigating options for long-term preservation.

UK Central Government Web Archive

The UK Central Government Web Archive is a selective collection of UK government websites developed by The National Archives of the UK (TNA).[21] The programme was initiated in 2003, and currently contains over 4,500 websites. These sites are collected by remote harvesting, either under contract by the Internet Archive and, since 2005, the European Archive, or directly by TNA using the UK Web Archiving Consortium's PANDAS system. A small number of sites are additionally acquired by direct transfer. TNA adopts a selective collecting policy, using a combination of specific and thematic criteria. All sites are freely accessible online, and long-term preservation facilities are provided through TNA's in-house digital preservation service. The programme is described in detail in the case study at the end of Chapter 9, Managing a Web Archiving Programme, and in examples elsewhere within the book.

UK Web Archiving Consortium

The UK Web Archiving Consortium (UKWAC)[22] comprises six UK organizations – the British Library, The National Archives, the National Libraries of Wales and Scotland, JISC and the Wellcome Trust – which have established a shared web archiving infrastructure, currently based on the National Library of Australia's PANDAS system. UKWAC was established in 2003, and uses selective collection via remote harvesting, including some thematic collections. UKWAC is described in detail in Chapter 9, Managing a Web Archiving Programme.

European Digital Archive

The European Digital Archive was established in Amsterdam in 2004 as a non-profit foundation.[23] Intended as an open archive for the public, its primary focus is web archiving, although it also collects multimedia material which is in the public domain. It maintains technology-sharing and collection-peering agreements with the Internet Archive, and acts as a technological partner for cultural institutions wishing to undertake web archiving. Using technologies developed by the Internet Archive and the IIPC (see below), it offers both highly focused and large-scale domain collection, using remote harvesting. It can also provide quality assurance, hosting, backup and long-term preservation of collections, with an online public access interface.

Summary: the spread of web archiving

These examples illustrate the diversity of the web archiving programmes that have been developed, in terms of both scale and approach. They demonstrate that successful web archiving can be undertaken by organizations of all sizes, from major national libraries and archives to consortia and university departments. Most have adopted a single collection method – remote harvesting – but implemented on a wide variety of technical infrastructures, from single workstations to multi-terabyte server arrays. They also illustrate a range of motivations for engaging in web archiving activity. In some cases, for example national cultural memory institutions, this derives from a clearly defined remit, such as legal deposit or archival legislation. Others, such as DACHS, are guided by a particular area of scholarly interest. Consortia such as the Nordic Web Archive and UKWAC have successfully combined a range of partners with very different depths and breadths of interest. The motivating factors are most apparent for those initiatives which have clearly defined collecting policies and typically adopt a more selective approach. The rationale for larger-scale, whole-domain harvesting approaches is sometimes, perhaps understandably, less apparent. The possible approaches to selection, and their articulation with particular curatorial traditions, are discussed in detail in the Chapter 3, Selection.

Collaboration: the IIPC and beyond

It is a sign of the growing maturity of web archiving as a discipline that these diverse initiatives are increasingly delivering benefits beyond their original confines, as international collaboration increases. Perhaps the most significant recent development has been the establishment of the International Internet Preservation Consortium (IIPC).[24]

The IIPC was founded in 2003 and, in many ways, represents the convergence of international web archiving initiatives, such as those previously described. The consortium currently comprises 12 partners: the national libraries of Australia, Canada, Denmark, Finland, France, Iceland, Italy, Norway and Sweden, the British Library, the Library of Congress and the Internet Archive. Although its current membership is restricted to the library community, the IIPC plans to extend this to other kinds of cultural heritage organization in future, in recognition of the wider interest in web archiving. The IIPC's stated mission is:

- to enable the collection of a rich body of internet content from around the world to be preserved in such a way that it can be archived, secured and accessed over time
- to foster the development and use of common tools, techniques and standards that enable the creation of international archives
- to encourage and support national libraries everywhere to address internet archiving and preservation.[25]

It is in the development of common tools and standards that the IIPC looks set to deliver the most immediate benefits. It has established a number of working groups to investigate specific topics, as follows:

- **The Framework Group** will develop a common technical architecture, standards for archival formats and metadata schemes and standard interface specifications, to enable interoperability between systems using the IIPC toolkit.
- **The Researcher Requirements Group** is investigating the requirements of users of archived web content, to determine how current selection

policies may influence future research and how future policies can be improved to address the needs of users better.

- **The Access Tools Group** will investigate the requirements for tools to access web archives over both the short and the long term.
- **The Metrics and Testbed Group** will develop a testbed for evaluating web archiving tools and processes, together with metrics for assessing their performance.
- **The Deep Web Group** will develop strategies and tools for archiving the deep web – that is, web content which is inaccessible to web crawlers.
- **The Content Management Group** will work on developing a unified and complementary approach to collecting policy among the consortium members.

Within this framework, various projects are being undertaken to create specific deliverables. The early focus of these has been the development of an open-source web archiving toolkit. Many of the components of this toolkit are based on earlier work by partner institutions.

To illustrate the breadth and depth of the envisaged toolkit, it is instructive to review the tools being developed by IIPC in 2005-6:

1 Heritrix is an open-source, archival quality web crawler for undertaking large-scale web harvesting. Initial development was carried out by the Internet Archive, to create a replacement for the existing Alexa crawler. The Nordic national libraries are now contributing to this project, based on their own experience of developing archival crawlers such as Combine, and the NEDLIB Harvester.

2 DeepArc is a tool for archiving relational databases, as a means of capturing deep web content. The tool enables the structure of a relational database to be mapped to an XML schema, which can then be used to export the database content into an XML document. DeepArc has been developed by the Bibliothèque nationale de France.

3 WARC (Web Archiving File Format) is the successor to the original ARC format developed by the Internet Archive. WARC includes a number of enhancements, such as support for richer metadata and

globally unique identifiers. WARC is supported by Heritrix, and potentially by other web crawlers in the future.

4   BAT (BnFArcTools) is an application programming interface (API) which allows developers to write tools to manipulate data stored in the ARC, DAT and CDX formats produced by Heritrix and the Internet Archive's original web crawler. BAT has been developed by the Bibliothèque nationale de France.

5   WERA (Web Archive Access) provides an access interface for web archives. Based on the NWA Toolset, it is comparable to the Wayback Machine. WERA is being developed by the National Library of Norway and the Internet Archive.

6   NutchWAX (Nutch with Web Archive Extensions) is a search engine for web archives, based on the existing open-source Nutch search engine. NutchWAX can be used to provide a search facility for access tools such as the Wayback Machine and WERA. It is being developed by the Nordic Web Archive and the Internet Archive.

7   Xinq (XML Inquire) is a tool for accessing XML databases, such as those collected using DeepArc. It provides search and browse access, and can allow the original functionality of an archived database-driven website to be recreated. Xinq is being developed by the National Library of Australia.[26]

Additional tools are planned for automating and prioritizing web crawls, and for managing the archival workflow. Many of the IIPC tools are described in more detail in later chapters. One of the most significant features of this work is that the individual tools are open source, and developed within a common framework. As such, they should prove of practical benefit to a wide variety of organizations wishing to engage in any or all aspects of web archiving.

The current and planned work of the IIPC gives grounds for considerable optimism. Certainly, the challenges of collecting and accessing web content are being very positively addressed. If other major issues, such as long-term preservation, receive equally well-directed attention, and if research can keep pace with new developments in web technology, then there is every reason to believe that major benefits will result.

Notes and references

1 The site can now be accessed within the historical section of the World Wide Web Consortium's website at www.w3.org/history/19921103-hypertext/hypertext/www/theproject.html [accessed 19 February 2006].

2 Quoted from the home page of the Internet Archive's website at www.archive.org/ [accessed 19 February 2006].

3 Mohr, G. et al. (2004) *An Introduction to Heritrix: an open source archival quality web crawler*, The Internet Archive, www.crawler.archive.org/An%20Introduction%20to%20Heritrix.pdf [accessed 1 November 2005].

4 See www.capricorn-tech.com/index.html [accessed 19 February 2006].

5 See Appendix 1 for further information on the open-source implementation of the Wayback Machine.

6 See www.bibalex.org/english/initiatives/internetarchive/web.htm [accessed 19 February 2006].

7 See http://combine.it.lth.se/ [accessed 19 February 2006].

8 See Appendix 1 for further information about WERA.

9 See http://netarchive.dk/ [accessed 19 February 2006].

10 See www.nb.no/paradigma/ [accessed 19 February 2006].

11 See http://pandora.nla.gov.au/ [accessed 19 February 2006].

12 See Appendix 1 for further information about PANDAS.

13 See www.nla.gov.au/initiatives/persistence.html [accessed 19 February 2006] for further information on the NLA's persistent identifier scheme.

14 See Appendix 1 for further information about HTTrack.

15 See http://mercator.comm.nsdlib.org/ [accessed 19 February 2006].

16 See www.kb.nl/coop/nedlib/ [accessed 19 February 2006].

17 See www.bnf.fr/ [accessed 19 February 2006].

18 See www.loc.gov/minerva/ [accessed 19 February 2006].

19 See www.sino.uni-heidelberg.de/dachs/ [accessed 23 November 2004].

20 See http://warp.ndl.go.jp/ [accessed 19 February 2006].

21 See www.nationalarchives.gov.uk/preservation/webarchive/ [accessed 19 February 2006].

22 See www.webarchive.org.uk/ [accessed 19 February 2006].

23 See www.europarchive.org/ [accessed 19 February 2006].

24 See www.netpreserve.org/ [accessed 19 February 2006].

25 See www.netpreserve.org/about/mission.php [accessed 19 February 2006].
26 See Appendix 1 for further information about Heritrix, DeepArc, BAT, WERA, NutchWAX and Xinq.

Chapter 3
Selection

Introduction

The initiation of any web archiving programme is self-evidently based on a decision to collect, which in turn implies the application of an explicit or implicit process of selection. The development of an appropriate selection policy is therefore an essential precursor to the implementation of any such programme. The nature of a given selection policy will be determined by a number of factors, including the remit and mission of the collecting organization, intellectual property rights issues and the institutional resources available. Web archiving programmes may be implemented by a wide variety of institutions, including libraries, archives, museums, research organizations, learned societies and commercial organizations, which may collect web resources for many diverse reasons, such as for their intellectual, evidential or artefactual qualities. Web archiving can therefore encompass many different curatorial traditions and approaches to selection.

It might appear that, within such well-established curatorial traditions, the development of selection policies for websites would pose no significant new issues, and it is certainly not the purpose of this chapter to discuss the general principles of appraisal and selection. However, the very nature of the world wide web challenges these traditions, and must be taken into account. These challenges arise from the structural, temporal and informational qualities of the web.

One of the principal defining qualities of the web is its interconnectedness. Every website has the potential to link to and be linked to from any number of other websites. It may also derive a greater or lesser part of its content from external sources, such as Really Simple Syndication (RSS) feeds. Indeed it is often difficult, if not impossible, to define any given website in terms of absolute boundaries. The facility to create, copy and link to information content with great rapidity renders obsolete the paper paradigm of discrete, enumerable and physically locatable information objects. It may in fact be more helpful to regard a website as a conceptual grouping of information experienced by a user, rather than as an artefact with any coherent physical existence. Furthermore, no website can be considered as an isolated object – it exists within a wider context which, ultimately, extends to encompass the entire world wide web. The breadth and complexity of that context is further complicated by its frequent opacity, whereby the relationships between resources may not be easily apparent. This poses self-evident problems for any selection policy, which necessitates the definition of boundaries, and the identification of some form of clearly delineated object that can be collected. It also raises more fundamental archival issues, in terms of the nature and authenticity of the material collected.

The web is also characterized by change: the 2001 study noted in Chapter 1, Introduction, suggested the average lifespan of a web page as being between 75 and 100 days, while other research has found that 44% of websites available in 1998 could no longer be found in 1999.[1] A longitudinal study of web page persistence, which has periodically monitored a sample of web pages between 1996 and 2003, has established an average 'half life' of two years; in other words, over a two-year period 50% of web pages will disappear.[2] The ease with which information may be presented and altered creates a uniquely transitory environment, whereby the content of a web page is likely to change on a regular basis. Thus, selection decisions about when and how frequently to collect may have a very significant impact on the nature of the resultant collection. In addition, an increasing proportion of web content is generated dynamically from databases, often customized to individual users. In such cases, there may be no 'definitive' view of a web page that can be identified and captured.

Finally, the nature of much of the informational content of the web defies traditional categorization. Although concepts such as 'publication', 'record' and 'artefact' can still hold true in some cases, such distinctions are increasingly becoming blurred, or even meaningless. The persistence of these concepts within an online environment can, arguably, be considered a reflection of its cultural immaturity, and part of a broader phenomenon in which the creators and users of IT systems seek reassurance in the retention of traditional paradigms that may no longer hold true. In any event, entirely new genres of information, such as blogs and wikis, are constantly emerging, demanding new approaches to selection.

This chapter describes a model process for making selection decisions, the context in which selection decisions must be taken, possible approaches to selection, selection criteria and the elements required to create a selection list.

The selection process

The selection process can be broken down into a number of discrete stages, which are illustrated in Figure 3.1.

Policy definition

First, a selection policy must be developed. A well-defined selection policy is an essential foundation for any web archiving programme. The exact nature of the policy will clearly vary according to individual organizational requirements, but its formulation will typically require the following steps:

• definition of context: the selection policy must be placed within the context of relevant external selection policies, any appropriate higher-level organizational policies and any analogous existing internal selection policies

• selection method: a number of possible approaches may be taken to selection, and an appropriate method must therefore be identified

• selection criteria: the policy must include well-defined selection criteria, capable of allowing specific selection decisions to be made.

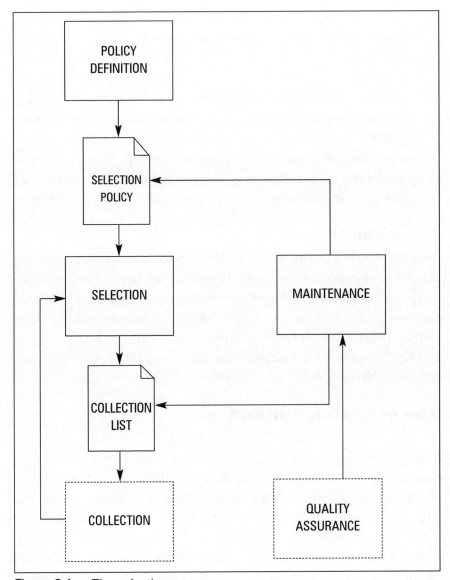

Figure 3.1   The selection process

Selection

Once the selection policy has been established it must be enacted, resulting in the selection of specific web resources for collection. This will be articulated in the form of a collection list, which is the end product of the selection process, and provides the basis for undertaking the actual collection of the resources. The collection list will need to address the following:

- boundary definition: given the interconnected nature of web resources, the boundaries of every resource on the collection list must be clearly defined
- timing and frequency: the appropriate timing and frequency of collection for each resource must also be specified; this should include a risk assessment methodology, if appropriate.

Maintenance

Typically, a web archiving programme will operate a continuous cycle of selection and collection, and both the selection policy and collection list will need to be maintained to ensure their currency. This may be refined through feedback of the results from the pre-collection quality control process (see Chapter 5, Quality Assurance and Cataloguing).

The remainder of this chapter discusses each stage of the selection process in detail.

The selection context

Over the past decade, web archiving has emerged as an issue of major concern to a wide variety of organizations on an international scale. It is therefore important that individual organizational selection policies should also be viewed within the global context. It is unlikely that any one organization will ever have the capability or desire to undertake truly comprehensive collection of the world wide web. It has previously been asserted that the interconnected nature of the web has fundamental implications for the context and completeness of every web resource collected for archival purposes. However, these issues may be addressed to a greater or lesser extent by the development of collaborative and complementary selection policies. In such a scenario, the web resources held within one web archive may depend on other resources held by an external archive to provide certain contextual information and even content. Thus, an external link from an archived website (which might otherwise be unactionable) could link to an archived copy of the appropriate site collected by another organization at the same time.

It may be questioned whether such a scenario is practical. Every organization with a curatorial mandate bases its selection decisions upon the perceived requirements of a defined constituency of users. Such constituencies are, to a greater or lesser extent, local to that institution. As such, selection policies are typically driven by local demand rather than a sense of global good.[3] However, models for such collaborative behaviour are already beginning to emerge within certain domains. For example, the UK Web Archiving Consortium (see Chapter 2, The Development of Web Archiving) is developing collaborative selection policies which both address the requirements of individual member institutions and complement those of others. This should help to eliminate the duplication of effort, and allow the development of a virtual web archive which is greater than the sum of its parts. Similarly, the International Internet Preservation Consortium (see Chapter 2, The Development of Web Archiving) is providing a forum for national libraries to collaborate on an international scale. Although the vision of a truly global, virtual web archive, containing every web resource deemed worthy of permanent preservation, remains unrealized and may never be truly achievable, such initiatives give cause for optimism that selection policies can exist within a context broader than organizational boundaries.

A web archiving selection policy may also have to be formulated in the context of an existing organization-wide selection policy, or analogous selection policies for other types of resource. For example, a library may have an existing selection policy for periodical publications, with which the new policy will be required to articulate.

An understanding of the broader context within which the selection policy will operate is therefore an essential precursor to the formulation of the policy itself.

Selection methods

A number of different approaches to selection are possible, which may be categorized according to their scope. Every selection method entails some degree of trade-off between the breadth and depth of collection.

Choices may be constrained by resource issues, including the collection technologies available to the collecting organization (see Chapter 4, Collection Methods).

Unselective

One approach is to take a conscious decision not to select, but rather to collect everything possible. This approach is exemplified by the work of the Internet Archive (see Chapter 2, The Development of Web Archiving), and is based on four main arguments. First, as previously discussed, the interconnected nature of the web means that the complete context for any given website ultimately encompasses the entire web, and can therefore only be preserved by collecting everything. Second, it is argued that selection is an expensive and time-consuming process, and that it is therefore simpler and more efficient to avoid specific selection decisions. Third, any process of selection is, by definition, subjective, and prejudges the importance that will be attached to specific resources by future generations. It can be argued that the unselective approach is entirely objective, and does not constrain the possible requirements of future researchers. Finally, it has been argued that it is technically feasible to collect everything, as demonstrated by the Internet Archive through the 'whole web' crawls it has been undertaking since 1996. However, it must be noted that even the Internet Archive is not currently able to collect the entire content of the world wide web – the 'deep web', which comprises information stored in databases and discoverable only by direct querying, is estimated to be 500 times larger than the surface web,[4] and currently remains largely inaccessible to its crawlers. Furthermore, such large-scale harvests take weeks to perform, during which time web content is continually changing or disappearing, and the notion of collecting a comprehensive, point-in-time snapshot of the whole web is therefore illusory. In addition, the Internet Archive acknowledges that such unselective collection should be complemented by more focused and selective collection methods, which deliver a greater depth and quality of collection.

The unselective approach is also possible within more limited contexts, such as national domains. For example, the National Library of Sweden has been undertaking unselective harvesting of the entire Swedish web domain since 1996 (see Chapter 2, The Development of Web Archiving). However, such an approach does in fact entail a limited degree of selection, since it requires the scope of the domain to be defined. This introduces some subjectivity – for example, the Swedish national domain can be defined as every site within the '.se' domain, every site hosted on a web server located within Swedish territory, every site managed or created by Swedish citizens or organizations or every site containing material related to Sweden.

The unselective approach may also have legal implications, if undertaken in a context where permission to collect is required. These are explored in Chapter 8, Legal Issues.

Thematic

An alternative is to define thematic selection criteria. This may be considered a semi-selective approach, since every resource within that theme could potentially be collected. A variety of thematic approaches can be envisaged, including:

1 Subject: Selection may be based upon subject matter, including events and topics. For example, the Digital Archive of Chinese Studies (DACHS) project is collecting social and cultural resources from the Chinese web (see Chapter 2, The Development of Web Archiving), and the Library of Congress has undertaken a number of thematic collections relating to U.S. presidential elections and the events of 9/11 (see Chapter 2, The Development of Web Archiving).

2 Creator: Selection may be determined by the individual or organization responsible for creating or managing a resource, such as a publisher or government agency.

3 Genre: The scope of selection may be based upon specific genres of resource, such as publications, blogs, web art or government records.

4 Domain: Scope may be defined in terms of specific web domains, such as '.uk' or '.edu'. It should be noted that the term 'domain' is used here in a sense that extends beyond the purely technical: for example, the UK government domain encompasses websites in a variety of web domains, including '.gov.uk', '.org.uk' and '.co.uk'.

A benefit of this method is that it may constrain the scope of collection to a more manageable size than the unselective approach. It is also likely that, by collecting all thematically related resources, some of the most significant context of each resource will be preserved.

Automated methods to support this approach are being developed. For example, the IIPC is developing the concept of a 'smart' web crawler for thematic collection, which uses sophisticated search and web page ranking techniques to identify resources for collection within a defined thematic area (see Chapter 4, Collection Methods).

Selective

The most narrowly defined selection method is to identify specific web resources for collection, such as a single web publication or website. This approach is exemplified by the National Library of Australia's Pandora programme (see Chapter 2, The Development of Web Archiving). Selection at such a high level of granularity may be advantageous in terms of intellectual property rights management (e.g. where explicit permissions to collect are required), and is likely to facilitate a more detailed understanding of the properties and qualities of the individual resources collected, which will benefit other processes, such as quality assurance, cataloguing, preservation and delivery.

By definition, the greater the degree of selectivity employed, the more subjective the resultant collection will be, constraining the as-yet-unknown requirements of future researchers. In addition, selection defines implicit or explicit assumptions about the material that will not be selected and which may therefore be lost to posterity. This is already well understood within archival traditions, which are predicated on the principle of disposition through retention or destruction.

The collection of resources in isolation also magnifies the problem of preserving context. The selective approach therefore requires particular attention to be paid to the definition of boundaries (see 'Defining the Boundaries' later in this chapter), in order to ensure the collection of meaningful and complete resources.

Selection criteria

Once the appropriate selection method has been identified, this must be articulated as a set of specific selection criteria. These criteria must be sufficiently detailed to allow individual selection decisions to be made which can, in turn, be translated into a list of web resources to be collected. Specifically, they must address three issues: content, extent and timing/frequency.

Content

Criteria must be established to define the nature of the web resources eligible for selection, in terms of their intellectual content. The level of detail required will depend upon the chosen selection method: the unselective and thematic approaches require minimal additional criteria, whereas the selective approach will require greater elaboration.

Extent

Allied to this, it will be necessary to establish criteria for determining the extent of selected resources. For example, it may be stated that no external links from websites will be collected. Again, this is highly dependent on the selection method, with the greatest detail being required for selective approaches. This aspect will need to be further elaborated within the collection list, at which point detailed technical boundaries must be defined.

Timing and frequency

Principles for determining the timing and, if appropriate, the frequency of collection also need to be established. Certain resources may only be collected on a single occasion. Examples of this include specific issues of a serial web publication, or a website with a fixed lifespan, such as that from a public inquiry. However, given the dynamic nature of the web, many resources will be collected at periodic intervals.

Bearing in mind the fragile and transitory nature of web resources, collection should take place as soon as possible after the point at which the content has been deemed worthy of selection. The timing and frequency of collection of each selected web resource will need to be defined in the collection list. However, these may be influenced by a number of factors: lifecycle, rate of content change, risk assessment and topicality/significance.

Lifecycle

The nature of a web resource may be defined in terms of its active lifecycle, which may be open-ended or of limited duration. For example, many organizational websites may exist and evolve over an indefinite period, whereas certain event-based websites may have a planned completion point, after which the content becomes fixed and the website may even cease to be maintained.

Rate of content change

A web resource's content may be dynamic or fixed. For example, a typical website homepage will be updated on a regular basis, whereas a journal article will probably be published to the web in a finished form. The frequency with which web content changes can vary enormously. Some websites or individual web pages may remain static for months or even years, whereas others may change significantly several times per day. Koehler has also noted that the rate of content change and persistence may vary between different disciplines, domains and content types.[5] For example, electronic journal articles may be more persistent than the entries in a personal blog. The rate of change will therefore be an important factor in determining the frequency with which a resource should be collected.

Risk assessment

Web resources are subject to the same processes of technological obsolescence that affect all types of electronic information, and therefore face the same risks that technological change will render them inaccessible (see Chapter 6, Preservation). Other risk factors may be financial (e.g. the termination of funding for a project-based website) or organizational (e.g. when a change in organizational priorities leads to particular web resources being removed or not maintained). An assessment of these risks should therefore inform the selection process. In some cases, such as websites managed by institutions with a high degree of organizational permanence, the risks may be judged to be negligible, although this should not necessarily be assumed. However, risk monitoring and assessment can provide invaluable insights to inform collection timings and frequencies.

Risk monitoring may, of necessity, be an informal process. However, if risk is considered an important factor, the selection policy should define the types of risk to be monitored, the means by which this will be achieved and a rationale for assessing the impact of that risk on specific resources. For example, the name and version of the web server software being used to host a particular website can be identified through analysis of the HTTP headers generated by the site. Equally, automated tools can be used to monitor the availability of a website, and track the frequency and duration of any downtime. The use of outdated web server software or the occurrence of frequent periods of downtime could be indicators of poor management practices and therefore signify a high degree of risk.

Risk assessment plays an important part in the long-term preservation process, and both methodologies and actual services are beginning to emerge to support this (see Chapter 6, Preservation).

In some cases, these can also be applied in the context of selection. One example is Cornell University's Virtual Remote Control (VRC) project,[6] which has developed a methodology for assessing and mitigating risks to live web resources. The VRC risk management framework defines a methodology for identifying, evaluating and appraising web resources of interest, developing a risk monitoring strategy and detecting and responding to risks. In parallel with this, the project is identifying and evaluating tools that can be used to implement the framework.

Topicality and significance

A major factor in determining the frequency of collection may be a subjective assessment of the topicality or underlying significance of a given resource. For example, the National Archives collects the majority of UK government websites on a biannual basis. However, for the duration of the Iraq conflict in 2004, it prioritized websites related to defence and foreign policy for high-intensity collection at weekly intervals.[7]

Defining the boundaries

Once the selection policy is implemented, it will generate a list of web resources to be collected. This list may be contained within the selection policy itself, if it is relatively static, or exist as a freestanding document, if it is highly dynamic. The list represents the articulation of the selection policy at a technical level, and must be actionable using the relevant collection method (see Chapter 4, Collection Methods). As such, it must define the boundaries of each selected web resource in sufficient detail to allow it to be collected.

Web resources are defined in terms of a uniform resource locator (URL), which provides a unique address for that resource within the world wide web. A URL comprises the following elements:

- scheme: http://
- domain name: www.nationalarchives.gov.uk/
- path: preservation/webarchive/default.htm.

The scheme defines the format of the URL, which will typically use a communication protocol such as the hypertext transfer protocol (HTTP) or the file transfer protocol (FTP).

The domain name defines the host for the web resource. This comprises two or more labels, separated by dots ('.'), and is read from right to left. The rightmost label is the top-level domain, which specifies either a country code (such as 'uk' for the United Kingdom) or a generic domain (such as '.com' for a commercial organization). The label to the left of this defines the second-level domain, which will generally either describe the hosting organization (e.g. 'microsoft.com') or define a generic domain to qualify a country code (e.g. '.gov.uk'). Labels to the left of this may be used to define further domain and subdomain levels. A fully qualified domain name also includes the host name of the web server, using the leftmost label. Thus, in the above example, the host name is 'www'.

This domain name must be translated into an internet protocol (IP) address, which uniquely identifies each host computer on the internet. This translation is performed by a domain name system (DNS) server, which maintains a concordance of domain names and IP addresses.

The path specifies the location of the web resource within the directory structure of the host web server, and is read from left to right. The URL may also optionally include a set of query parameters to be passed to an underlying database, for example in order to generate a web page dynamically on a database-driven website.

Thus, in the example above, the URL points to a file called 'default.htm', located within the directory path 'preservation/webarchive/', hosted in the 'nationalarchives.gov.uk' domain on the 'www' host web server.

The boundaries of a web resource will typically be defined in terms of either a URL or a domain name, optionally qualified by a set of parameters. If a single web resource, such as a web page or a document, is to be collected in isolation, then the collection list would simply need to specify the URL of that resource (e.g., www.mypublisher.com/publications/book1.pdf). However, if an entire website, or subset of a website, has been selected this will usually be defined as a domain name, and optionally a path, which contains all of the resources to be collected (e.g., 'www.nationalarchives. gov.uk').

Certain parameters will usually be required to qualify this. The nature of these will depend upon the collection method being employed. However, typical parameters would define the number of levels of the directory structure to be collected, and whether or not external links should be followed and, if so, to what depth.

Particular care must be taken to ensure that the domain is correctly identified. For example, websites may use a number of different host names, such as 'www1' and 'www2', which can provide access to different content. Identification of the appropriate host name or names is therefore essential. Websites may also include subdomains, which might not be collected unless they are explicitly identified. For example, the website 'www.uktradeinvest.gov.uk' includes two major subdomains, 'www.trade. uktradeinvest.gov.uk' and 'www.invest.uktradeinvest.gov.uk'. Most collection methods will not capture these unless specifically configured to do so.

The definition of the boundaries of a specific resource may require some analysis of the live resource, and should be reviewed as part of pre-collection quality assurance (see Chapter 5, Quality Assurance and Cataloguing).

Timing and frequency of collection

The collection list must also define the timing and, if appropriate, the frequency with which each selected web resource is to be collected. This should be determined in accordance with the factors described in 'Selection Criteria' earlier in this chapter, and will need to be regularly reviewed as part of the maintenance of the list. For example, the perceived topicality of a website will almost certainly change over time, requiring an adjustment to the collection frequency.

Four basic scenarios are possible: repeated, ad-hoc, one-off or comprehensive collection.

Repeated collection

It may be necessary to collect a web resource at repeated intervals. This approach will typically be applied to dynamic resources with open-ended lifecycles. The most pragmatic approach to capturing changes will usually be to collect a series of static 'snapshots' of the resource over time. In such a scenario, the frequency with which the resource is sampled becomes a critical factor. Typical frequencies might be weekly, six-monthly or annually. In addition, consideration must be given to whether subsequent collections should be incremental or total – that is, whether to capture only the content that has changed, or to recapture the entire resource. This decision may well be determined by technical considerations relating to the collection method (see Chapter 4, Collection Methods).

Ad-hoc collection

Web resources may change at unpredictable rates. Where this is the case, repeated collection at a fixed frequency may prove inefficient, resulting in the repeated collection of the same content. An alternative approach is to collect in response to a trigger event, such as some form of automated or manual monitoring of the resource or an alert from some external source. For example, the DACHS project (see 'Selection Methods' in this chapter) makes significant use of human informants to identify new material for collection.

One-off collection

In some cases, a specific web resource may be selected for collection on a one-off basis. This will typically apply to resources which have fixed content, such as an online publication. In additional, certain types of material may change over a set period of time, and then stabilize in a fixed form. An example would be the website for a government public inquiry, which may change rapidly while the inquiry is in progress and new content is being added, but will then become fixed once the inquiry has published its findings. In such cases, it may be considered appropriate to collect the site only once it has become fixed. However, it should also be borne in mind that, if the changes are significant, or material is being removed as well as added, repeated collection may also be required during the dynamic stage of the resource's lifecycle.

Comprehensive collection

On occasion, it may be necessary to capture the complete lifecycle of a dynamic and open-ended web resource. This is essentially a special case of the one-off approach, and is most likely to be required in a records management environment where online transactions need to be preserved for evidential purposes. In such cases, collection for archival purposes will need to be integrated within the website management workflow. This is probably the least commonly applied selection approach, but methodologies for achieving this have been developed (see 'Transactional Archiving' in Chapter 4, Collection Methods).

Maintenance

The selection policy should not remain static, but must be updated to reflect changes in internal and external factors, such as new organizational priorities and developments in the world wide web itself. Equally, the collection list, whether a part of the policy or not, will clearly be dynamic. Feedback from the collection and quality assurance of web resources should be used to refine the selection process. For example, as resources are collected, new resources may be identified that need to be considered for selection. There may also be more pragmatic lessons to be learned; the availability of organizational resources and infrastructure, including specific strengths or limitations of the available collection technologies which may be revealed, could require revisions to the selection approach.

It is therefore essential that the selection policy include procedures for maintaining the currency of the policy, for translating selection decisions into updates to the collection list and for approving and implementing changes. The regularity with which such maintenance needs to be undertaken will depend upon the selection method adopted, and the frequency of collection: a web archiving programme which is engaged in high-frequency collection will probably need to review its policies more frequently than one that only undertakes episodic collection.

Summary

The size, diversity, interconnectedness, ephemerality and multifaceted nature of the web all contribute to the potential difficulties of selecting and identifying web content to be archived. It is therefore essential that any web archiving programme is based on a robust and clearly articulated selection policy. Many different approaches to selection are possible; however, whichever approach is adopted – unselective, thematic or selective – it must take into account both the requirements of the collecting organization, and the characteristics of the web resources to be collected. It must allow the definition of an identifiable set of web resources for collection, with clearly defined boundaries and collection frequencies. Finally, the selection policy must be maintained and updated on a regular basis, to ensure its continuing relevance and fitness for purpose. A clearly defined and well maintained selection policy is the cornerstone of any web archiving programme, and an essential prerequisite for building a coherent and meaningful collection.

Notes and references

1   Lyman, P. (2002) Archiving the World Wide Web. In *Building a National Strategy for Digital Preservation: issues in digital media archiving*, Council on Library and Information Resources Report, 106, 38–51, www.clir.org/pubs/reports/pub106/pub106.pdf [accessed 23 November 2004].

2   Koehler, W. (2004) A Longitudinal Study of Web Pages Continued: a
     consideration of document persistence, *Information Research*, **9** (2),
     http://informationr.net/ir/9-2/paper174.html [accessed 16 February
     2006].

3   This argument was advanced by Abby Smith, Director of Programs with
     the Council on Library and Information Resources, in a keynote address
     at the 'Archiving Web Resources' international conference hosted by the
     National Library of Australia in Canberra, November 2004.

4   Bergman, M. K. (2001) The Deep Web: surfacing hidden value, *Journal of
     Electronic Publishing*, **7** (1), www.press.umich.edu/jep/07-01/
     bergman.html [accessed 23 November 2004].

5   Koehler, W. (2004) A Longitudinal Study of Web Pages Continued: a
     consideration of document persistence, *Information Research*, **9** (2),
     http://informationr.net/ir/9-2/paper174.html [accessed 16 February
     2006].

6   See the VRC website at http://irisresearch.library.cornell.edu/VRC/
     index.html [accessed 23 November 2004] for further information.

7   The National Archives (2003) Operational Selection Policy 27: the
     selection of Government websites,
     www.nationalarchives.gov.uk/recordsmanagement/selection/pdf/
     osp27.pdf [accessed 29 October 2005].

Chapter 4

Collection methods

Introduction

This chapter describes various possible methods of collecting websites for archival purposes. The variety of approaches is dictated by the nature of web technology itself. This chapter therefore begins with a summary of website technology, before describing the various collection methods in detail. The strengths and limitations of each method are also considered. The design of a website can be an important factor in determining the ease with which it can be collected, and the range of methods appropriate. This chapter therefore also considers how webmasters can create 'archive-friendly' websites.

The technology of the web

The experience of using the world wide web arises from the interplay between two fundamental components – the web server and the web client, such as a web browser. A web server stores content, such as HTML pages and images, which it delivers, or 'serves', to a web browser in response to requests from that browser. A web browser requests content from web servers, and renders that received content for the user. The interaction between these two components is therefore as significant as the components themselves. Some form of communications protocol provides the mechanism by which this interaction takes place. The protocol defines a standard format for communications between the server and the browser. The most commonly used protocol on the web is the hypertext transfer protocol (HTTP). Thus, when a browser sends a request to a server, that request takes the form of an HTTP 'message', as does the reply from the server.

All the content available on a web server is identified using a uniform resource locator (URL) – a reference which describes where on the web that content is located (see Chapter 3, Selection, for a more detailed discussion of URLs). The nature of URLs is one of the defining characteristics of the web, and creates a very indirect relationship between browsers and servers. Neither the browser nor the server need to know anything about each other, beyond the information contained within the HTTP message. Thus, a browser requests content by sending an HTTP request containing the relevant URL. It does not know, or need to know, anything about the web server which physically hosts that content – the mechanism for translating that URL into a physical location happens while the request is en route, initially through the DNS resolution system (see Chapter 3, Selection) and finally through the processing of that request by the web server. Similarly, the server need only reply to that request, either with the requested content or, if the request cannot be fulfilled for any reason, with an appropriate error message.

The experience of using a website therefore arises from a series of 'transactions' between a web server and a web browser, which are constrained by the content available on that server. As a consequence of this, two alternative views of the nature of a website can be adopted. It may be considered that a website comprises the sum of its available content, and incorporates all possible transactions that could occur. On the other hand, it is equally possible to view a website purely in terms of the transactions that actually occur, and therefore limited to that subset of its content which is delivered in reality. These alternatives are reflected in the two fundamental categories of collection technique. Content-driven collection methods seek to archive the underlying content of the website, whereas event-driven approaches collect the actual transactions that occur. The appropriateness of one philosophy over the other, and the subsequent influence that this may have on the choice of collection method, will be determined by the curatorial tradition and selection policy of a given organization.

A further distinction can be made, based on the source from which the content is collected. It can be archived either from the web server (server-side collection) or from the web browser (client-side collection). The applicability of either approach is determined by another fundamental characteristic of website technology: websites can be categorized as being static or dynamic.

Static websites

A static site is made up of a series of pre-existing web pages, each of which is linked to from at least one other page. Each web page is typically composed of one or more individual elements. The structure and textual elements will typically be contained within an HTML document, which contains hyperlinks to other elements, such as images, and to other pages. All of the elements of the website are stored in a hierarchical folder structure on the web server, and the URL of each element describes its location within that structure.

The target for a hyperlink is normally specified in the 'href' attribute of an HTML element, and defines the URL of the target resource. The form of the URL may be absolute (a fully-qualified domain and path name) or relative (only including the path name relative to the source object). These can be illustrated in the following examples:

> Absolute:
> ```
> <A href="http://www.mysite.com/products/new.html">New
> Products</A>
> ```
>
> Relative:
> ```
> <A href="new.html">New Products</A>
> ```

Relative links are considered best practice, both for ease of website management and, from an archival perspective, because they greatly ease the complications of rewriting the links in archived websites to remain functional within their archival environment.

Dynamic websites

In a dynamic site, the web pages are generated 'on the fly' from smaller elements of content. When a request is received, the required elements are assembled into a web page and delivered. Types of dynamic content include:

1   Databases: The content used to create web pages is often stored in a database, such as a content management system, and dynamically assembled into web pages.
2   Syndicated content: A website may include content which is drawn from external sources, such as RSS feeds and advertising pop-ups, and then dynamically inserted into the web page.
3   Scripts: Scripts may be used to generate dynamic content, responding differently depending on the values of certain variables, such as the date, type of browser making the request, or the identity of the user.
4   Personalization: Many websites make increasing use of personalization, to deliver content which is customized to an individual user. For example, cookies may be used to store information about a user and their previous visits to a website. These cookies are stored on the user's computer, and returned by their browser whenever they make a request to that website.

Depending on the nature of a dynamic website, these 'virtual' web pages may be linked to from other pages, or may only be available through searching. Websites may contain both static and dynamic elements. For example, the homepage, and other pages that only change infrequently, may be static, whereas pages which are updated on a regular basis, such as a product catalogue, may be dynamic. The presence of dynamic content which is only discoverable through searching places a fundamental constraint on the available collection methods. Client-side methods cannot be used, since collection of all the available content would require the submission of every possible search request. Server-side methods are therefore the only viable approach in such cases.

The range of possible methods for collecting web content is dictated by these considerations. Four alternative collection methods are currently available, which can be categorized in a matrix as shown in Table 4.1. Each of these methods is discussed in detail in the following sections.

Table 4.1   The matrix of collection methods

	Content-driven	Event-driven
Client-side	Remote harvesting	No method available
Server-side	Direct transfer Database archiving	Transactional archiving

Direct transfer
Overview

Conceptually, the simplest method of collecting web resources is to acquire a copy of the data directly from the original source. This approach, which requires direct access to the host web server, and therefore the co-operation of the website owner, involves copying the selected resources from the web server and transferring them to the collecting institution, either on removable media such as CD, or online using e-mail or FTP.

Direct transfer is most suited to the acquisition of static websites, which simply comprise HTML documents and other objects, stored in a hierarchical folder structure on the web server. The whole, or a part, of the website can be acquired simply by copying the relevant files and folders to the collecting institution's storage system. The copied website will function in precisely the same way as the original, with two provisos. First, the hyperlinks within the website must be relative links in order to continue functioning correctly – if this is not the case then it is a comparatively simple matter to convert absolute links to relative ones. Second, any search functionality included in the original website will no longer be operable unless the appropriate search engine is installed in the new environment.

Dynamic websites which rely on an underlying database to provide content are more problematic to collect by this method. In these cases, the database or content management system will need to be installed in the archival environment, together with the necessary web server and search engine software. This has major resource implications: licences will be required for all the software components, full technical documentation will be required from the original website to allow the system to be recreated, and staff with the appropriate technical skills must be available to install and maintain the system. In addition, that system must then be maintained in the long term, which will present a substantial preservation challenge (see Chapter 6, Preservation). Furthermore, many different combinations of database, web server and search engine technology are in use on the world wide web. For example, a survey of web servers in 2005 revealed over 150 variants of server software in significant use (i.e. in use on more than 1000 websites each), although the market is dominated by four types of platform.[1]

This diversity extends even to the level of the operating system: various versions of Unix, Windows and Linux are all widely used. Every website acquired in this manner is therefore likely to require the recreation of a different supporting technical environment. The maintenance of such a diverse IT infrastructure is almost certainly unsustainable.

The issues involved with the direct transfer approach can best be illustrated through two case studies.

Case study: Number 10 Downing Street

The very first website to be collected by The National Archives of the UK (TNA) was a snapshot of the Number 10 Downing Street website taken on 6 June 2001, the day before a general election (see Figure 4.1, overleaf). This was a database-driven website, powered by a content management system, and was transferred to The National Archives in the form of database back-up tapes. These tapes were then used to reinstall the database and website onto a web server hosted by The National Archives, involving substantial work by a number of technical staff. The website was successfully rebuilt and made available for public access. However, changes to the TNA website and IT infrastructure in 2004 meant that the content management system could no longer be easily supported. To provide continued public access, the website was therefore harvested with a web crawler (see 'Remote Harvesting' below) to generate a static version that did not require a database or any specific web server technology. Although providing much valuable experience, this demonstrated that the archiving of database-driven websites in their original form was not a viable option for TNA.

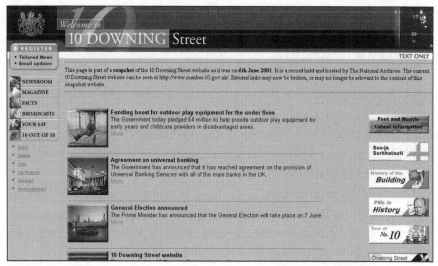

Figure 4.1   The No. 10 website in 2001 (Crown Copyright)

Case study: Bristol Royal Infirmary Inquiry

TNA continues to collect some static websites by direct transfer, in particular those which have lifecycles of limited duration. In such cases, a single copy of the website will be collected at the end of its lifecycle. An example of this is the website from the Bristol Royal Infirmary Inquiry (see Figure 4.2). The Inquiry web team made a copy of the complete website folder structure, which was then transferred on CD to The National Archives and accessioned into its digital archive. A website such as this does not require any specific operating system or web server technology; the only aspect of its functionality that has not been preserved is the site search facility, which used a specific search engine technology. However, searching is a comparatively simple function to replace (see Chapter 7, Delivery to Users).

Strengths

The principal advantage of the direct transfer method is that it potentially offers the most authentic rendition of the collected website. By collecting from source, it is possible to ensure that the complete content is captured, with its original structure. In effect, the collecting institution re-hosts a

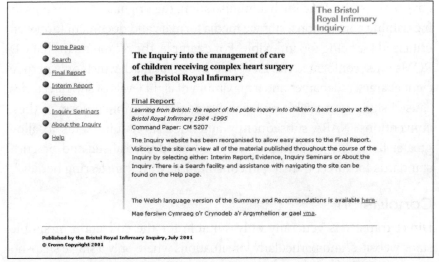

Figure 4.2   The Bristol Royal Infirmary Inquiry website (Crown Copyright)

complete copy of the original website. The degree of authenticity which it is possible to recreate will depend upon the complexities of the technical dependencies, and the extent to which the collecting institution is capable of reproducing them.

Limitations

The major limitations of this approach are the resources required to effect each transfer, and the sustainability of the supporting technologies. These limitations are much more evident for dynamic websites. In addition, this method requires co-operation on the part of the website owner, to provide both the data and the necessary documentation. As the amount of work entailed is likely to be proportional to the complexity of the website, this is again likely to be a greater issue for dynamic websites. The potential problems faced when using direct transfer were highlighted in 2001 when the National Archives and Records Administration in the United States (NARA) required all federal agencies to produce snapshots of their websites at the point of presidential transition between the Clinton and Bush administrations. In addition to the timescale, which required all snapshots to be created and transferred to NARA within 60 days of the start of the Bush administration, the original requirements for file naming conventions, storage media formats and documentation were criticized for being too inflexible. For example, the requirement that CD-ROMs must conform to the ISO 9660-1990 standard, which only permits eight-character filenames and a maximum of eight levels of sub-directories, caused significant problems for websites that did not conform to these conventions. NARA subsequently amended its requirements to allow greater flexibility, underlining the need to adopt realistic and practical standards for direct transfer, in consultation with transferring bodies.[2]

Conclusion

Direct transfer is generally only suitable for the collection of simple, static websites, and particularly for situations where only a single snapshot is required. The one exception to this might be if a collecting institution's selection policy is limited to websites utilizing a common technological environment: in such cases, it might be feasible to collect dynamic websites by this method. However, this method is manual and resource-intensive, and depends upon the active participation of the website maintainers. Consideration should therefore be given to other methods, which may yield equally good results more efficiently.

Remote harvesting
Overview

Remote harvesting is the most widely employed method for collecting websites. It involves the use of web crawler software to harvest content from remote web servers.

Web crawlers belong to a broad family of software collectively referred to as 'robots' or 'spiders'. Robots are software programs designed to interact with online services as though they were human users, principally to gather information. Among the most common robots are the tools used by search engines such as Google to collect and index web pages.

A web crawler shares many similarities with a desktop web browser: it submits HTTP requests to a web server and stores the content that it receives in return. The actions of the web crawler are dictated by a list of URLs (or seeds) to visit. The crawler visits the first URL on the list, collects the web page, identifies all the hyperlinks within the page, and adds them to the seed list. In this way, a web crawler that begins on the homepage of a website will eventually visit every linked page within that website. This is a recursive process, and is normally controlled by certain parameters, such as the number of levels of hyperlinks that should be followed.

The infrastructure required to operate a web crawler can be minimal: the software simply needs to be installed on a computer with an available internet connection and sufficient storage space for the collected data. However, in most large-scale archiving programmes, the crawler software is deployed from networked servers with attached disk or tape storage devices.

Background

There is a wide variety of web crawler software available, both proprietary and open-source. Although it is not the purpose of this book to describe the detailed operation of any specific tool, mention should be made of the three most widely used web crawlers: HTTrack, the NEDLIB Harvester and Heritrix.

HTTrack was developed by Xavier Roche (see Appendix 1). Although originally developed as a generic offline browser, it has been one of the most widely adopted crawlers for web archiving purposes over a number of years, being used by a number of major initiatives, including the National Library of Australia's Pandora programme. However, in the future it seems likely that it will increasingly be replaced by purpose-built archival crawlers such as Heritrix. HTTrack is best suited to the focused collection of specific websites in small-scale crawls.

An archival-quality crawler was developed collaboratively by a number of European national libraries, as part of the Networked European Deposit Library (NEDLIB) project (see Chapter 2, The Development of Web Archiving). It has been widely used in a number of major web archiving programmes, including the Nordic Web Archive and the Finnish EVA project. However, development of the software ceased in 2002, and it is no longer maintained or supported. The majority of institutions using the NEDLIB Harvester are now planning to replace it with Heritrix. The

NEDLIB Harvester was designed specifically for undertaking whole-domain crawls.

Heritrix has been developed jointly by the Internet Archive and the Nordic Web Archive as the next-generation archival-quality web crawler. Its continued development is being taken forward under the auspices of the International Internet Preservation Consortium (see Chapter 2, The Development of Web Archiving and Appendix 1). Heritrix is suited to a wide range of selection methods, from large-scale, whole-domain crawls to the capture of individual websites.

The IIPC is also developing a 'smart web crawler' based on Heritrix. Designed to automate thematic selection approaches, this crawler will use page analysis to identify content for archiving. Through a combination of thematic analysis and link weighting, the crawler will automatically identify and prioritize content to collect against a defined selection policy. The thematic analysis will comprise a suite of techniques for classifying the content of a web resource, including keywords and word frequency analysis. Link weighting measures the significance of a web page in terms of the number of links to that page, and the significance in turn of each of those links. This approach lies at the heart of the Google search engine's 'page rank' scoring, and has been demonstrated to provide an effective measure of a page's relevance to a particular theme.

The development of this smart crawler is being driven by the requirement to undertake continuous crawling. Traditionally, focused crawling has required detailed manual creation of collection lists and setting of crawl parameters, which is time-consuming and limits the size and frequency of the crawls that can be undertaken. Equally, large-scale, domain-level crawls typically take several months to complete, and therefore can only be repeated at limited intervals. The development of a crawler capable of continuous harvesting, with automated selection and prioritization requiring only limited manual intervention, is therefore very significant. Such a crawler can essentially be left to run on an ongoing basis, continually collecting new content within its defined thematic area.

Although not itself a web crawler, the National Library of Australia's PANDAS system (see Chapter 2, The Development of Web Archiving) provides workflow capabilities that allow user control of the overall collection process, including permissions tracking, cataloguing, crawler configuration and quality assurance.

Parameters

Web crawlers provide a number of parameters which can be set to specify their exact behaviour. Many crawlers are highly configurable, offering a very wide variety of settings, as illustrated in Figure 4.3. Although the details will vary according to the specific web crawler software, most crawlers will provide variations on the following parameters: connection, crawl, collection, storage and scheduling settings.

Connection settings

These settings relate to the manner in which the crawler connects to web servers:

1   Transfer rate: The maximum rate at which the crawler will attempt to transfer data (usually expressed in kilobytes per second). This will, in practice, be limited by the available bandwidth. This setting is important, as the use of a high setting may impose a serious load on

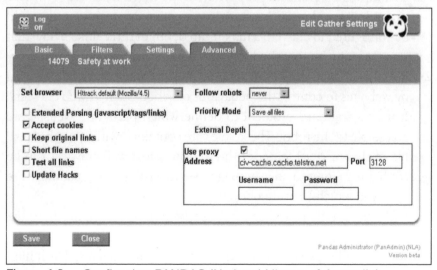

Figure 4.3   Configuring PANDAS (National Library of Australia)

the website being crawled. Equally, it may be possible to specify a minimum transfer rate, to ensure that data is captured at a sufficient rate to enable an entire site to be collected in a reasonable timescale.

2   Connections: It may be possible to specify the number of simultaneous connections the web crawler can attempt to make with a host, or the delay between establishing connections. This is an important factor in minimizing the load on the host.

Crawl settings

These settings allow the user to control the behaviour of the crawler as it traverses a website, such as the direction and depth of the crawl.

1   Link depths and limits: This will determine the number of links that the crawler should follow away from its starting point, and the direction in which it should move. It should also be possible to determine the limits of the crawl, in terms of whether or not the crawler is restricted to following links within the same path, website or domain, and to what depth. This is important to prevent the crawler from collecting too broadly – owing to the interconnectedness of websites, if no such limits were imposed then the crawl could rapidly encompass a significant proportion of the world wide web. Thus, for example, a crawler starting from 'www.nationalarchives.gov.uk' could be configured to crawl to a maximum depth of three links below that starting point, and limited to URLs within the '.gov.uk' domain.

2   Robot exclusion notices: A robot exclusion notice is a method used by websites to control the behaviour of robots such as web crawlers. It uses a standard protocol to define which parts of a website are accessible to the robot. These rules are contained within a 'robots.txt' file in the top-level folder of the website. Most web crawlers can be configured either to obey or to ignore these rules, or to customize the extent to which they are obeyed.

3   Link discovery: The user may also be able to configure how the crawler analyses hyperlinks: these links may be dynamically constructed by scripts, or hidden within content such as Flash files, and therefore not transparent to the crawler. However, more

sophisticated crawlers can be configured to discover many of these hidden links.

Settings will normally be available to control the size and duration of the crawl. For example, it may be desirable to halt a crawl after it has collected a given volume of data, or within a given timeframe.

Collection settings

These settings allow the user to fine-tune the behaviour of the crawler, and particularly to determine the content that is collected. Filters can be defined to include or exclude certain paths and file types: for example, to exclude links to pop-up advertisements or to collect only links to PDF files. Filters may also be used to avoid crawler traps, whereby the crawler becomes locked into an endless loop, by detecting repeating patterns of links. The user may also be able to place limits on the maximum size of files to be collected.

In cases where the same website is to be collected on a repeated basis, it is redundant to collect content that remains unchanged between harvests, as this will result in duplication. Some crawlers can be configured to recognize previously harvested content which remains unchanged. This process, which is sometimes known as 'adaptive revisiting', involves the initial collection of a complete snapshot of the website. On each subsequent visit, only new and updated content is collected, and each subsequent snapshot is therefore incrementally built upon its predecessors. This method is clearly more efficient in terms of crawling time and storage space.

Storage settings

These settings determine how the crawler stores the collected content. By default, most crawlers will mirror the original structure of the website, building a directory structure which corresponds to the original hierarchy. However, it may be possible to dictate other options, such as forcing all images to be stored in a single folder. These options are unlikely to be useful in most web archiving scenarios, where preservation of the original structure will be considered desirable.

The crawler may also be configured to rewrite hypertext links, for example to convert from absolute to relative path names.

Scheduling settings

Tools such as PANDAS, which provide workflow capabilities, allow the scheduling of crawls to be controlled. Typical parameters will include:

1   Frequency: The frequency of collection can be defined, for example daily or weekly.
2   Dates: The user may be able to specify the date on which the schedule should commence.
3   Non-scheduled dates: It may also be possible to define specific additional crawl dates, to be executed in addition to the standard schedule.

Identifying the crawler

Software agents, such as web browsers and crawlers, identify themselves to the online services with which they connect through a 'user agent' identifier within the HTTP headers of the requests they send. Thus, Internet Explorer 6.0 identifies itself with the user agent `Mozilla/4.0` (`compatible; MSIE 6.0; Windows NT 5.1`). The user agent string displayed by a web crawler can generally be modified by the user. This can be advantageous for three reasons.

First, it allows the crawler to identify itself as being controlled by a particular institution's web archiving programme. Thus, for example, The National Archives' web crawlers use the user agent `Mozilla/5.0` (`compatible; tna_crawler +http://www.nationalarchives.` `gov.uk/reservation/webarchive/webmasters.htm`) - this identifies the crawler and provides a link to a web page containing general information about TNA's crawling activities, together with contact details for more specific enquiries. This approach is highly recommended: the user agent details will be recorded in the server logs of any crawled website, and therefore provide a transparent first point of contact for any webmaster who wishes to find out more information.

Second, web servers may be configured to block certain user agents, including web crawlers and search engine robots. For example, some websites will block the default HTTrack user agent `Mozilla/4.5` `(compatible; HTTrack 3.0x; Windows 98)` to prevent unauthorized copying of their content. Defining a more specific user agent can prevent such blocking, even if using a crawler that would otherwise be blocked.

Finally, some websites are designed to display correctly only in certain browsers (principally Internet Explorer), and check the user agents in any HTTP request accordingly. User agents which do not indicate the correct browser compatibility will then be redirected to a warning page. To avoid web crawlers being similarly redirected when attempting to archive such a site, the crawler's user agent can be redefined to mimic an IE-compatible browser.

Harvesting dynamic content

Web crawlers can, in principle, collect any content to which a link can be discovered. The limitations on collecting dynamic content through remote harvesting have been previously described, and arise principally in the following circumstances:

- where links cannot be discovered by the crawler because they are dynamically generated (for example, with JavaScript), or otherwise hidden
- where content is not directly linked, and is only discoverable through a user search.

Even these limitations may be overcome in some cases through new technologies such as Google Sitemaps. Google search robots can crawl URLs that would not otherwise be discoverable. An XML Sitemap file, containing a list of URLs available to be crawled, can be generated automatically from web server logs, directories or pre-existing URL lists using a variety of tools. The Sitemap can include additional information about each URL, such as its priority for crawling or frequency of updating, to allow intelligent crawl decisions to be made. There is no reason why, in principle, the same technique could not be used to control archival web crawlers. However, the generation of a Sitemap does require administrative access to the web server which is to be crawled, which limits the value of this method.[3]

Aside from these issues, web crawlers are perfectly capable of collecting dynamically generated content. Irrespective of how a web page is created, it is always delivered to a web browser as a standard HTTP message, which is therefore amenable to collection by a harvester. However, the process of remote harvesting has the effect of 'flattening' dynamic content into static pages, so that the dynamic behaviour is lost. This can have advantages, since static websites are typically simpler to manage and preserve. Collecting organizations will need to determine on a case-by-case basis whether any such loss of behaviour is significant.

Strengths

The greatest strengths of remote harvesting as a methodology are its ease of use, flexibility and widespread applicability, together with the ready availability of a number of mature software tools. A remote harvesting programme can be established very quickly, and allows large numbers of websites to be collected in a relatively short period.

The methodology is proven, and a large body of experience is available internationally. The infrastructure requirements are relatively simple, and it requires no active participation from website owners: the process is entirely within the control of the archiving body. Most web crawler software is comparatively straightforward to use, and can be operated by non-technical staff with some training, although more sophisticated tools, such as Heritrix, do require a greater degree of technical literacy.

In short, remote harvesting offers the simplest route for an organization to begin web archiving, and certainly yields the highest productivity of any collection method.

Limitations

The large volumes of data that can be collected through remote harvesting, and the speed with which they can be acquired, can also be seen as a limitation: if the other parts of the web archiving process are unable to cope with this throughput then a backlog can quickly accumulate.

Although web crawling tools can be simple to use, the best results can only be achieved through careful configuration. Fine-tuning crawlers can, at times, be something of a black art, and a wrongly configured crawler can cause considerable damage. For example, a crawler which is set to establish the maximum possible number of simultaneous connections to a web server, and use all the available bandwidth to download content, can have a very serious impact on the performance of the web server being crawled, or even cause it to crash completely. It need hardly be said that it is vital to ensure that archival crawling does not affect the operational performance of the website being archived.

However, the greatest limitation of the remote harvesting method is its inability to collect certain kinds of dynamic content. For example, documents which are only retrievable through searching cannot be remotely harvested, and crawlers may be unable to discover and follow links which are dynamically generated, or contained within binary objects such as Flash content, resulting in a failure to capture the linked content.

Database archiving
Overview
Remote harvesting is of limited use for collecting dynamic, database-driven websites. At best, it will collect a static version of a site, in which the interactive elements of behaviour have been lost; at worst, it will be unable to collect any content. The increasing use of web databases has made the development of new web archiving tools a priority, and such tools are now beginning to appear.

The process of archiving database-driven sites involves three stages: first the repository defines a standard data model and format for archived databases; then each source database is converted to that standard format; and, finally a standard access interface is provided to the archived databases.

This allows the use of generic access tools, and removes the need to support varied, possibly proprietary, database technologies.

The obvious technology to use for defining archival database formats is XML, which is an open standard specifically designed for transforming data structures. Several tools now exist for converting proprietary databases to XML formats. These include SIARD, developed by the Swiss Federal Archives, and the Bibliothèque nationale de France's DeepArc software.

Both tools allow the structure and content of a relational database to be exported into standard formats. SIARD automatically analyses and maps the database structure of the source database. It then exports the definition of the database structure as a text file, containing a data definition described using SQL, the international standard for defining relational database structures; the content is exported as plain text files, together with any large binary objects stored in the database, and the metadata is exported as an XML document. The data can then be reloaded into any relational database management system to provide access.

DeepArc enables a user to map the relational data model of the original database to an XML schema, and then export the content of the database into an XML document. It is intended to be used by the database owner, since its use in any particular case requires detailed knowledge of the underlying structure of the database being archived. First, the user creates a 'view' of the database. An XML schema is used to create a skeleton, describing the desired structure of the XML document that will be generated from the database. The user then builds associations to map the database to this view. This entails mapping both the database structure (i.e. the tables) and the content (i.e. columns within those tables). Once these associations have been created and configured, the user can then export the content of the database into an XML document which conforms to the defined schema. If the collecting institution defines a standard XML data model for its archived databases, it can therefore use a tool such as DeepArc to transform each database to that structure.

Both tools can, in principle, be connected to any relational database.[4] However, it should be noted that they are relatively complex, technical tools to use, and require detailed knowledge of relational database design and XML.

Strengths

The principal advantage of this method is quite clear: it offers a generic approach to collecting and preserving database content, which avoids the problems of supporting multiple technologies incurred by the alternative approach of direct transfer. This limits issues of preservation and access to a single format, against which all available resources can be brought to bear. For example, archives can use standard access interfaces, such as that provided by the Xinq tool (see Chapter 7, Delivery to Users).

Limitations

Web database archiving tools are a recent development, and are therefore still technically immature compared to some other collection methods. Support for specific database technologies is also currently limited, which constrains the number of websites to which this approach can be applied. Both of these limitations are likely to be overcome as the technology develops and matures.

Database archiving also raises questions about the nature and timing of collection. As a dynamic resource, the content of databases is likely to change on a regular basis. The issues of defining an appropriate selection policy for such resources have been explored in Chapter 3, Selection. At present, this approach allows one or more point-in-time snapshots of a database to be collected; changes to content between collection times may not be captured. As such, this approach may only be acceptable in certain circumstances.

The current database archiving tools do not preserve the original 'look and feel' of the website, which is an important consideration. This should therefore be regarded as a method for collecting database *content*, rather than database-driven *websites*. As such, its applicability will depend upon the requirements of the selection policy.

Finally, in common with the direct transfer method, this approach requires the active co-operation and participation of the website owner. Indeed, considerable work may be entailed on their part, to map the original database schema to the archive schema. Such an approach is therefore only possible if such co-operation is forthcoming.

Transactional archiving
Overview

Transactional archiving is a fundamentally different approach from any of those previously described, being event- rather than content-driven. It focuses on collecting the actual transactions that take place between the web server and the browser, rather than the content which is available to be delivered from the web server. In other words, it seeks to collect evidence of the actual use of the website, and the user experience provided, rather than the underlying content that contributes to that experience.

Its development as a methodology has been driven by the imperatives of accountability, evidential weight and regulatory compliance. There are a number of scenarios in which a website owner may wish, or be required, to provide evidence of the content which was either available, or actually accessed, at a specific point in time.

In the commercial sector, compliance with legislation such as the Sarbanes-Oxley Act and Basel II, together with other legal and regulatory requirements for the disclosure and retention of certain information for defined periods, may demand that a company be able to prove what information was available on its website on a given date (see Chapter 8, Legal Issues).

Websites are increasingly used to provide evidence of prior art, that is, all information that has been disclosed to the public in any form before a given date, especially to support applications for patents. There are many documented cases where both live websites and web archives, such as the Internet Archive, have been used to support or challenge patent claims. In such cases, the evidential requirement to demonstrate when web content was published is paramount.

More generally, any organization that publishes information on the web, especially information which expresses opinions, provides advice or represents significant intellectual capital, may require evidence of exactly what information was published on what date, to support or defend against possible legal action.

There may be a very significant difference between the content which was potentially available and that which was actually experienced, at any given moment. This may occur for a number of reasons, including:

1   Technical problems: Certain content may be unavailable at certain times due to technical problems, resulting in a user either receiving a '404 - Page not found' error or, more insidiously, only receiving part of the

content of a web page, perhaps being unaware that anything is missing.

2   Customization: websites and browsers offer increasing opportunities for content to be customized to individual users, using techniques such as cookies. For example, anyone who has registered on the Amazon website receives personalized web pages whenever they visit the site, including individual recommendations. Web browsers can also indicate a wide range of user-specific preferences in the HTTP requests that they submit to servers (see 'Migration on Demand' in Chapter 6, Preservation, for further discussion), which can result in different responses.

Furthermore, websites now draw on an increasingly wide range of information sources, many of which are outside their direct control, such as syndicated news feeds. This in turn means that there may be no single source of content to archive. As a result, the concept that a single, universal representation of a website exists is becoming increasingly simplistic. The concept of transactional archiving has been developed to address this.

The PageVault system provides a good example of an approach to transactional web archiving.[5] It monitors all requests which are submitted to a web server, and the responses which are returned. All responses that are identified as being 'materially different' are then archived. The definition of what constitutes a material difference can be modified, depending on the needs of the archiving organization.

PageVault comprises four components, as follows:

1   Filter: The filter intercepts pairs of queries and responses on the web server, and temporarily writes them to disk. It performs initial removal of duplicates but, because it does not have a global view of the system, and to minimize any impact on the performance of the web server, it will include many 'false positives'.

2   Distributor: The distributor reads the query/response pairs generated by the filter, and processes them to remove further duplicates. It then passes summary information to the archiver for further processing.

3   Archiver: The archiver maintains the permanent collection of materially different responses. Since it represents the total collection of unique

responses, it is able to perform the final filtering of duplicate responses based on the summaries received from the archiver. Once a response is identified as unique, the archiver requests the full response from the distributor, and adds it to the collection.

4   Servlet: The servlet provides an access interface to the contents of the archiver, allowing users to search and retrieve all archived content.

PageVault uses flexible, user-defined 'signatures' to determine non-material content. For example, a signature might be defined to filter out the displayed system time, or the contents of an online shopping basket, if variations in these are not considered a material difference. A checksum is then calculated for each server response, excluding those parts that have been identified as non-material. This checksum is then compared to the checksums for those responses which have already been archived, to determine whether this is a genuinely 'new' response.

Although transactional archiving does not allow search functionality to be preserved, it does capture how a website responded to specific user searches over time.

Strengths

The great strength of transactional archiving is that it collects what is actually viewed. As such, it offers the best option for collecting evidence of how a website was used, and what content was actually available at any given moment. For selection policies that emphasize the evidential value of websites, it is therefore a strong candidate. It also shares with remote harvesting the ability to collect what was delivered, irrespective of its source. It can therefore be a good solution for archiving certain kinds of dynamic website.

Limitations

By definition, transactional collection does not collect content which has never been viewed by a user. Depending on the underlying purpose of collection, this may or may not be an issue. However, by definition, unviewed content provides no evidence of user interaction. Unviewed static pages could therefore be equally well collected by remote harvesting, while the set of unviewed dynamic content is potentially infinite, and therefore uncollectable.

Because transactional collection takes place on the web server, it cannot capture variations in the user experience which are introduced by the web browser, if two browsers render the same content in slightly different ways. However, there is no obvious solution to this, and it is unlikely to be relevant in the vast majority of cases.

Transactional archiving must take place server-side, and therefore requires the active co-operation of the website owner. Although elements of the system might be distributed and shared, a local instance of at least the filtering mechanism will need to run on each web server being archived. As such, transactional archiving is only suitable for selection policies that require the repeated collection of a predetermined and relatively static list of websites.

Because they require intervention within the live request/response cycle of the web server, transactional archiving methods have an impact on the performance of the server. In other words, the time taken for the server to process and respond to each request will be longer. Although the performance impact may be nominal (for example, PageVault claims to add an average of 0.4 milliseconds to the total response time),[6] such a direct intervention within the operational environment may be unacceptable to the website owner, and will, at the very least, require careful negotiation.

Optimizing websites for archiving

Website owners can take a number of steps to facilitate the archiving of their website. In some cases, there may be a natural tension between operational business requirements and 'archivability'. For example, there may be a strong business need to use highly dynamic content, even though this dramatically increases the complexities of archiving. In most cases, archiving can be expected to be a low priority for the website owner, and the degree of influence which an archiving organization can exert on the owner will also vary greatly. For example, a national archive may expect to be able to influence the website management practices of government departments to some degree, but a national library cannot realistically place any requirements on private website owners.

Nevertheless, it is worth considering some basic steps that can be taken to make websites more 'archive-friendly'. Ideally, such considerations would influence the initial design of a website. However, they can usefully be implemented at any time.

Allowing archival access

The website should allow access to legitimate archival crawlers, as defined by their user agents, and should ensure that archival crawling is supported in any robot exclusion notice.

URLs and path names

Websites should always use relative rather than absolute path names for all hyperlinks. Even excluding archival considerations, this is good website management practice, and will greatly simplify routine maintenance.

Websites should use stable, persistent URLs, and have procedures in place to detect and remedy broken links. Stable URLs support citation of website content, whether formally (e.g. the many websites referenced in this book), by search engines or through the bookmarking of pages by users. If URLs vanish from a website, known as 'link rot', users will experience 'page not found' errors, which can damage an organization's reputation and cause loss of business.

Documentation

Webmasters should maintain full documentation of the technical architecture of the website, including all hardware and software dependencies. This can provide important provenance information about the website, and will be crucial when using direct transfer or other server-side collection methods. It can also help in the diagnosis of errors encountered during remote harvesting.

Metadata

All website content should include full and accurate metadata, such as standard Dublin Core metadata elements. This will not only improve the searchability of that content, and the accuracy of search results, but will also support the use of smart web crawlers to discover new content automatically for archiving.

Conclusions

This chapter has surveyed the range of alternative collection methods that are currently available, and highlighted the strengths and limitations of each. It can be concluded that no single method provides a universal solution for web archiving, and that a combination of techniques is required to deal with the full range of website technologies that may be encountered.

Client-side archiving is the most widely applicable, mature and easily applied collection method. Remote harvesting is by far the most common method in use, and has successfully achieved large-scale collection of content in a very wide variety of organizational settings, implementing a diverse range of selection policies.

Server-side archiving offers advantages for certain kinds of dynamic content, but requires the active participation of the website owner, and these methods are therefore of more specialized interest. Database archiving is currently the only viable method for collecting diverse database-driven websites and retaining their dynamic behaviour. It is also the only alternative to transactional archiving for collecting unlinked content which is only available through searching. It is therefore likely to be the collection method of choice in certain circumstances. However, as a relatively resource-intensive method, which requires both co-operation and time from the website owner, it is likely to be a relatively niche technique.

Like other server-side collection methods, transactional archiving is likely to be a technique of relatively specialist interest. Although not suitable for large-scale collection of multiple sites, it does offer unique advantages in special cases.

Direct transfer is only suitable for occasional use, and when restricted to static sites. Nevertheless, it can prove the simplest method for acquiring individual websites on a one-off basis.

A single web archiving programme will not necessarily make use of all four methods: this will be determined by the scope of the selection policy. Nonetheless, it is commonplace for a programme to use more than one technique in parallel, and to adopt different methods over time, to reflect changes both in selection and in the technologies being used by the target websites. A sound understanding of the collection methods available, and their strengths and limitations, is therefore essential to the success of any programme.

Notes and references

1   *Netcraft Web Server Survey*, November 2005
    http://survey.netcraft.com/reports/0511/ [accessed 19 February 2006].
2   For further information on the issues faced with the 2001 presidential
    snapshots see www.gcn.com/vol20_no3/news/3650-1.html,
    www.gcn.com/vol20_no5/news/3768-1.html and
    http://cio.doe.gov/rbmanagement/records/pdf/att1-01-11.PDF [all
    accessed 18 February 2006].
3   See www.google.com/webmasters/sitemaps/ [accessed 19 February 2006]
    for further information on Google Sitemaps.
4   Specifically, they both use the Java Database Connectivity (JDBC)
    interface to access the source database. JDBC drivers are available for
    most relational databases.
5   See Appendix 1 for more information about PageVault.
6   Fitch, K. (2003) *Website Archiving: an approach to recording every materially
    different response produced by a website*, Project Computing,
    http://ausweb.scu.edu.au/aw03/papers/fitch/ [accessed 19 February
    2006].

Chapter 5

Quality assurance and cataloguing

Introduction

Quality assurance is an essential component of any web archiving programme. All collection methods involve some degree of automation, and it is therefore vital to ensure that the selection policy and collection list are actually being implemented successfully. The nature and degree of quality assurance which is required or practical will depend upon the needs and resources of the collecting agency, and the selection approaches and collection methods employed. In general, the greater the scale of collection undertaken, the more basic the level of quality assurance that can realistically be employed. This dictates that there is invariably a trade-off between the number of resources that can be collected, and the quality control which can be applied to them, and a policy decision is required as to the minimum acceptable level of assurance.

Whatever the level of detail at which it is applied, any quality assurance process should follow the basic model illustrated in Figure 5.1 overleaf.

This chapter describes these processes in detail, and identifies some of the most commonly encountered problems and their possible solutions. It also discusses the cataloguing of archived websites. Some form of catalogue description is required in order to manage any archival collection, and make it accessible to users. Although cataloguing may take place at

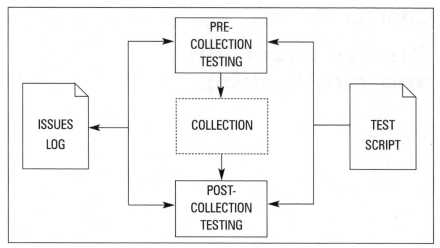

Figure 5.1   The quality assurance process

various stages in the web archiving process, it is included here because an important element of quality assurance is to ensure that all necessary cataloguing is accurate and complete.

Pre-collection testing

Pre-collection testing is concerned with the identification of potential issues that may affect the quality of collected content, in advance of its acquisition. It is clearly desirable to identify and resolve as many potential problems as possible prior to collection, thereby minimizing the extent of post-collection testing required. Pre-collection testing will typically include two approaches: resource analysis and test collection.

Resource analysis

This involves the manual or automated analysis of the target web resource, in order to identify the appropriate collection method and any issues that are likely to arise during collection. At the most basic level, it will be necessary to determine whether the website is static or dynamic in nature and, if the latter, whether all of the target resources are linked or only available through database queries. The website should also be investigated for obvious potential problems (see 'Common Issues' below), such as JavaScript-controlled menus or extensive use of Flash content. This analysis should determine whether the target resource is suitable for collection using remote harvesting, or if another method will have to be employed. An overview of the applicability of different collection methods for particular types of web resource is provided in Chapter 4, Collection Methods.

Test collection

If a target web resource is only intended to be collected on a single occasion then the next stage will be to undertake the actual collection. However, if it is intended that a resource will be collected repeatedly, it may be beneficial to undertake a test collection. This will allow the selected collection method to be fully evaluated, and any necessary corrections made to the collection parameters. The resource should be tested using the same techniques as for post-collection testing, which are described in the following section.

Post-collection testing

Some degree of post-collection testing is essential, to ensure that the selection policy and collection list are actually being enacted successfully. The extent of testing, however, is likely to vary considerably, being constrained principally by the volume of resources collected. In general, the most feasible approach will be to test a representative sample of the collected material, the size of the sample being determined by the volume of the collection and the available resources.

To ensure consistency, testing should always be based on a standard test script, which describes the precise tests to be conducted and allows recording of the results. The test script should be followed using two web browser windows, for both the live and the archive versions of the web resource: this allows valid comparisons to be made between the results. The following are examples of the types of test that may be required:

1   Availability: The most basic test is to ensure that a website snapshot has actually been captured and is available.
2   Navigation: The functionality of site navigation should be tested. General site navigation should be checked by attempting to navigate

between pages using the various available methods, including in-text hyperlinks, navigation bars, drop-down menus and buttons. Navigation methods which use scripts to create the hyperlink dynamically will need particular testing, since these links may be missed by web crawlers. To ensure that the full content has been captured, at least two levels of linking should be tested. It is particularly important to ensure that all navigation links to archived resources, rather than to the live website. This can be checked by referring to the URL displayed in the browser's address bar.

3   Date and time: If the website includes a date and time display, this should preferably be frozen at the time of capture.

4   Frames: If the website uses frames then a representative sample of pages should be checked to ensure that these display correctly in the archive version.

5   Text: The textual content of a representative sample of pages should be checked to ensure that it has been captured and displays correctly.

6   Images: If the website incorporates images then a representative sample of pages should be checked to ensure that these have been captured and display correctly.

7   Multimedia content: If the website includes multimedia content, such as audio and video, or animations and other dynamic resources using technologies such as Flash, a sample of these should be tested for functionality.

8   Downloadable content: If the website includes downloadable content, such as PDF files, a representative sample should be tested to ensure that the content has been captured and can be accessed.

9   Search: If the website includes a search facility then this should be tested using queries known to produce both positive and negative results. The search functions on websites collected using remote harvesting will almost certainly not be captured.

Further details of the typical causes of and solutions to the issues addressed by these tests are provided below in 'Common Issues'. A full sample test script, based on that used by The National Archives for weekly harvests, is provided in Appendix 3. As a basic benchmark, experience at The National Archives suggests that it is possible to test 10 harvested websites per person per hour, following this test script.

The International Internet Preservation Consortium (IIPC), and in particular the Bibliothèque nationale de France, is working to develop automated approaches to quality assurance for large-scale crawls, based on comparisons between the collection list and the actual URLs retrieved. These techniques should greatly enhance the ability of collection organizations to assure the quality of their archives.

Issue tracking

Testing at the pre- and post-collection stages may identify issues that need to be addressed, and an efficient system for logging, tracking and resolving those issues lies at the heart of the quality assurance process. Every issue identified must be recorded in a standard issue log, and include the following information:

- the nature of the issue, giving sufficient detail for it to be independently identified
- the severity of the issue, on a defined scale
- the date when it was identified
- the person who identified it
- the individual, organization or process identified as responsible for resolving the issue
- the date on which the issue was passed for resolution
- the expected resolution date.

Once the issue has been passed on for resolution, the log should be monitored periodically for outstanding issues, and any necessary action taken to facilitate their resolution.

Once the issue has been resolved, the following information should be recorded:

- the date on which the issue was resolved
- the manner in which the issue has been resolved

- an indication of whether the issue is now closed or, if the resolution is unsatisfactory, remains open.

It should be noted that the resolution of an issue does not necessarily imply that the underlying problem has been solved, but merely that no further action is required. For example, the issue may arise from the technical limitations of the collection method employed, and thus merely be noted.

Whether the issue tracking system is entirely manual, using paper logs, or uses specialist issue tracking software, the fundamental process is the same. In cases where another agency is involved in the issue resolution process (e.g. if a third-party contractor is responsible for collection), it may be necessary to include details of the issue tracking system in any contractual arrangements.

A sample issue log, based on that used by The National Archives, is provided in Appendix 4.

Common issues

A number of issues are commonly encountered during web collection, some of which are specific to particular collection methods whereas others are universal. In general, these have equally common solutions. An understanding of these common issues will improve the efficiency of any quality assurance process. The majority of the following issues relate primarily to resources collected using remote harvesting, although many will be equally applicable to other methods.

Incorrect navigation function and missing content

Problems relating to site navigation and missing content are essentially part of the same issue. Correct site navigation within an archived website requires two elements. First, the hyperlink must point to the correct target within the archived, as opposed to the live, website. Second, the target for the hyperlink must have been captured.

The target for a hyperlink is normally specified in the 'href' attribute of an HTML element, and defines the URL of the target resource. The form of the URL may be absolute (a fully-qualified domain and path name) or relative (only including the path name relative to the source object). A web crawler will be capable of following both types of link, assuming they are valid. However, without intervention, absolute links will remain unchanged in the captured version of the page, and thus will continue to link to the live version of the target. Relative links, on the other hand, will function correctly in the archived version. This can complicate the identification of missing content during quality assurance: the archive copy may appear to display correctly, because some elements are being retrieved from the live website, thus potentially masking whether or not they have actually been captured. Equally, content that appears to be missing may actually have been captured, but is merely no longer correctly linked.

This problem can be resolved by rewriting all hyperlinks to a relative form. Thus, a hyperlink of the following form:

```
<A href="http://www.mysite.com/products/new.html">New
Products</A>
```

could be rewritten as:

```
<A href="new.html">New Products</A>
```

The link rewriting can either be performed on a copy of the archived version, or dynamically through the archive presentation system, and is explored in more detail in Chapter 7, Delivery to Users.

A similar issue may occur when hyperlinks are either dynamically constructed using JavaScript, or embedded within objects such as Flash files: if these hyperlinks are of absolute form, they will continue to link to the live version. This problem is more difficult to resolve, as it would require a considerable degree of intervention to rewrite links of this type.

There may be a number of reasons why the target content of a hyperlink is not collected. One likely cause is that the linked content is hosted in a domain which was not specified in the collection list. For example, many websites store downloadable documents in a document repository, often hosted in a different domain from the main website. This can be verified by checking to see whether the URL for the content is within the scope of the current crawl parameters, and can obviously be rectified by changing those parameters as required.

A second possibility is that the crawler may be obeying a 'robots.txt' rule which excludes access to the folders containing the required content on the web server. This is a common reason for missing images: the 'robots.txt' file may include a rule to exclude the 'images/' folder or equivalent. The usual remedy for this will be to carry out a targeted recrawl of the relevant folders, ignoring the rule.

A major cause of missing content stems from the failure of the web crawler to identify and follow all of the hyperlinks within a web page. Dynamically constructed or embedded hyperlinks of the types mentioned above can be particularly problematical. A common example is the use of Flash-driven menus for navigation. Although the abilities of crawlers to extract the hyperlinks in such scenarios are continually being improved, hyperlinks of these types may well be inaccessible to them. As a result, the linked content will not be retrieved, and the navigation links will not function. Missing content of this type can usually be collected manually, after following the link on the live website to ascertain the correct target URL.

Finally, the content may be protected from either access or download, for technical, security or copyright protection reasons. Certain pages, or indeed entire websites, may be password-protected. These can be collected by configuring the web crawler to provide the necessary password information. Download protection, which enables content to be viewed in a browser but not copied, can be more problematical. This issue most commonly affects images and multimedia content, including Flash animations. In many cases, the simplest solution may simply be to obtain copies of the content directly from the owner. The same solution applies to material which cannot be retrieved for technical reasons. For example, Java applets reside on the host web server and are simply called from within a web page; as such, they will not be captured by crawling.

Text-only version of a website collected

This issue only affects remote harvesting approaches, and occurs when websites offer both graphical and text-only versions to users. In some cases, the text-only version will automatically be supplied if the user's browser is identified by the web server as being 'unsupported'. This most typically applies to browsers other than Internet Explorer and Netscape Navigator. In the same way, a web crawler may be misidentified as being an unsupported web browser. This issue can be solved by changing the web crawler's user agent to mimic that of a supported web browser (see 'Identifying the Crawler' in Chapter 4, Collection Methods).

Multilingual content

Websites may support multilingual access by providing alternative language versions of the same content. Multilingual content is usually selected via a link which either runs a server-side script to deliver an alternative set of pages, or uses a cookie to store a language preference. Without additional control, a web crawler will tend to retrieve pages in a random mixture of languages. Additionally, the language toggle on the archived website is unlikely to function. It is difficult to reproduce this facility in an archived version, since it requires recreation of server-side functions, and the simplest option is therefore to collect separate snapshots of the website for each language version. This can be achieved by either configuring how the crawler manages cookies, or by targeting the crawler specifically to follow or avoid the language toggle link on the home page.

Multimedia content

Streaming audio and video may well not be captured using remote harvesting methods, and dynamic content such as Flash is often protected against download. Often the only solution may be to obtain copies of the resources directly from the content owner.

Date/time display

Many web pages display the current date and time. It is generally desirable for the archived version of the page to display the date/time at the time of capture. However, in some cases it may be found that the current values are displayed instead. The reasons for this will depend upon how the date/time display is generated in the web page. The display will normally be generated using a JavaScript function; the crucial factor is how and when this function is run. If the function is run by the web server as the page is being generated, the resultant page will simply include the value returned by the function, and will therefore remain fixed in the archived version. If the function executes after the web page has been generated, the function itself will be captured in the archived version, and will be executed whenever the page is opened. Usually, the function will return the current system date and time for the server from which it is being generated: thus, the archived version will always display the current date. In a few cases, the function may instead use a set of variables generated by the web server at the time of generation; since these variables will be captured in the archived version, the date of harvesting will be preserved. In a few cases, the current date and time may continue to display because they are contained in a separate frame of the web page which has not been captured, and which therefore continues to be fetched from the live website. In the latter case, the problem may be solved by widening the scope of the crawl to include the relevant frame. Otherwise, these issues cannot easily be resolved.

Cataloguing

Any collection of archived websites requires some form of catalogue description. This is necessary both to enable proper management and to support access by users. Organizations which are creating web archives as part of wider pre-existing collections will almost certainly wish to integrate these websites with their existing catalogues. Libraries, archives and museums all have their own cataloguing traditions, and it is beyond the scope of this book to discuss the details of how websites may be catalogued within each such tradition. Nevertheless, it is worth noting that major cataloguing standards, such as MARC 21 and ISAD(G),[1] have been successfully applied to the description of archived websites.

Whichever standard is to be applied, three main issues need to be considered:

- the level of cataloguing required
- the catalogue metadata to be captured
- how that metadata will be captured.

Traditional approaches to cataloguing tend to be time-consuming and resource-intensive. As such, they may be unsuitable for web archiving programmes which are generating large volumes of archived sites. Certainly, the chosen cataloguing process will need to be sustainable for the collection method in use. Two extremes of catalogue detail are evident in current practice. The minimal approach is exemplified by the Internet Archive (see Chapter 2, The Development of Web Archiving), which captures very little metadata about each archived snapshot beyond the date of harvesting, and restricts its cataloguing entirely to metadata that can be automatically generated. This is the only feasible approach for the volumes involved. At the other end of the spectrum, programmes such as Pandora (see Chapter 2, The Development of Web Archiving) take a much more traditional library approach, whereby each website is manually catalogued in some detail. This sits most easily within highly selective collection strategies, where the number of sites being harvested is strictly limited. However, it should be noted that the sophistication of automated cataloguing techniques is rapidly improving, thanks largely to the advent of archival-quality web crawlers such as Heritrix. The IIPC is pioneering this approach which, coupled with the capture of detailed information from HTTP headers during crawling, can generate a much greater volume of metadata useful to the archivist.

The types of metadata to be captured will depend partly on the cataloguing standard in use. However, beyond the purely descriptive metadata, certain technical metadata will be required to support ongoing management and long-term preservation (see 'Preservation Metadata' in Chapter 6, Preservation). This will need to include details of the time and technical method of collection.

For much of the more traditional, descriptive metadata, there is no substitute for manual creation. However, the scope for automatic capture of metadata is increasing. Websites may include metadata encoded within their HTML pages, using standards such as Dublin Core. In such cases, it is possible to extract that metadata during or after collection. For well-documented websites, this can provide the basis for a descriptive catalogue record: for example, Dublin Core metadata may describe the creator, date, title, content and other important attributes. However, such metadata should be treated with a degree of caution: re-use of existing web pages by webmasters as templates for creating new pages can result in the inadvertent retention of incorrect metadata. Technical metadata should certainly be amenable to automatic generation. For example, most web crawlers will produce detailed logs describing a specific harvesting operation.

The timing at which cataloguing is performed will also vary. In selective approaches, where the websites to be collected are all identified in advance, it is usual for outline catalogue records to be created in advance of collection. Systems such as PANDAS (see Chapter 2, The Development of Web Archiving) support this within their workflows. In such cases, additional cataloguing and quality assurance are then conducted post collection. For less selective approaches, catalogues may be constructed almost entirely from automatically generated metadata, with only minimal human intervention, perhaps to create the top-level records.

The need for detailed descriptive metadata is somewhat reduced by the advent of increasingly sophisticated full-text search engines. The impact of these is discussed in more detail in Chapter 7, Delivery to Users.

Summary

Quality assurance and cataloguing are two vital stages in the workflow of any web archive. They ensure that the selection policy is being implemented correctly, and that collected content is described adequately to support its long-term preservation and use. Collecting web content is a complex process, and no method can be guaranteed to provide perfect results. Testing prior to collection maximizes the efficiency of the collection process, and reduces potential quality issues from the outset, while post-collection testing ensures the quality of the collected content.

Cataloguing is a further means by which the quality and fitness-for-purpose of archived material can be enhanced, and a variety of standards and levels of detail can be adopted to suit different needs. The level of quality assurance and cataloguing undertaken should always be appropriate to the nature of the content, and the requirements and available resources of the collecting organization. The proper use of such measures will play a vital role in creating a reliable and useful web archive.

Reference

1   International Council on Archives (ICA), *ISAD(G): General International Standard Archival Descriptions*, 2nd edn, 2000.

Chapter 6

Preservation

Introduction

This chapter provides an overview of the principles and practicalities of preserving archived web content over long periods of time. Digital preservation is a new and rapidly evolving discipline: the first comprehensive analysis of digital preservation as a global issue was only published in 1996[1] and, although significant advances have been made since then, mature solutions to the challenges are only now beginning to appear.

Preserving digital objects over long time periods presents a number of complex challenges, and a detailed discussion is beyond the scope of this book. This chapter discusses the major issues, and the key functions required to deliver a preservation service. These functions are common to the preservation of all types of digital content – the approach described can be applied equally to websites or anything else. Where web content does introduce particular issues, these are discussed at the end of the chapter.

The challenge of digital preservation

The purpose of preservation is to ensure the continued accessibility of an object over time, such that the inherent qualities of the object which merited its collection are maintained. In other words, successful preservation requires that the object be accessible to users, and that it retain its intrinsic value to those users. In the world of traditional collections, the principal obstacle to preservation is entropy. Physical materials suffer damage and decay: the acids present in paper damage its fibres, causing it to become brittle and discoloured over time; colour dyes in photographic films and prints continue to be chemically active, fading through exposure to light or high temperatures. Such concerns also apply to digital objects: the physical storage media will degrade over time, or may become corrupted. However, digital preservation must also overcome a unique and much more significant challenge – that of technological obsolescence.

Digital information is stored in the form of bits – ones and zeros which denote values in binary notation. These bits have no inherent meaning, but rather represent the encoding of information in accordance with some predefined scheme. Such information cannot be directly interpreted by a user, but rather requires the mediation of software capable of translating that information into human-readable form. To illustrate this, Figure 6.1 shows a small segment of a digital image encoded in the common TIFF file format, with the byte values expressed in

Figure 6.1   Encoding of a digital image

hexadecimal notation. The values of the bytes in this segment have meaning only in the context of the published specification for the TIFF format[2] – in this case they represent the colour values of individual pixels at specific locations within the image – and require the intervention of software capable of decoding TIFF images to render them into a meaningful image.

This same image could be converted to another image format, such as GIF. At the bit level, the object would be fundamentally different, as GIF encodes the same information according to a different specification. However, to the user both files would still render an identical image. Thus, a level of abstraction always exists between the information content of a digital object and its encoding, which can only be bridged through the application of the appropriate technologies. Moreover, multiple technologies are required. Our example TIFF image requires appropriate image rendering software; the software will require a particular operating system and hardware configuration to run; and the operating system will have its own hardware requirements too. The storage medium on which the image is stored will require an appropriate drive to read it, which will in turn have further hardware and software requirements. Thus, it can be seen that access to a digital object depends upon a complex network of interconnected technologies; this network is known as a 'representation network', since it comprises all of the elements required to represent the object correctly. The absence or failure of any part of this network will potentially render the object inaccessible.

However, technology is constantly changing and evolving. Information technology is a rapidly advancing field, with new and improved technologies regularly being developed. Equally, market forces place pressure on technology developers to follow a regular cycle of product replacement, offering new products, and new versions of existing products, on a frequent basis. The pace of change is exemplified in the manufacture of semiconductors: the number of transistors that can be fitted onto an integrated circuit, which offers a rough guide to computer processing power, has broadly doubled every 18 months since the 1970s, an effect known as Moore's Law. Similar levels of exponential growth apply to hard disk storage space per unit cost.

As new products are brought to market, existing products cease to be supported. The currency of a given technology is therefore typically very short – perhaps five to ten years. This rapid rate of obsolescence applies to all technologies in the representation network, including file formats, software, operating systems and hardware. The challenge of digital preservation therefore lies in maintaining the means of access to digital objects in the face of rapid technological obsolescence. In particular, it requires methods for identifying and predicting the impacts of technological change on digital collections, and for executing appropriate preservation strategies to mitigate them.

However, maintaining access in itself is not enough. The definition at the beginning of this section referred to preserving the intrinsic value of the object as well – in archival terms, this means preserving the authenticity of the record. The nature of authenticity for objects which are subject to frequent and fundamental change is a complex and vigorously debated subject, and is beyond the scope of this book. The crucial fact is that different curatorial traditions demand varied approaches to authenticity – the archival, library and museum communities must separately determine the definition that meets their needs. However, a powerful framework for discussing these issues is provided by the 'performance' model, developed by the National Archives of Australia.[3] In this model, digital objects – the source – are rendered into a meaningful form – the performance – using one or more processes (the representation network). The critical element here is the performance, rather than the underlying objects: provided that the essential performance can be replicated over time, the particular source and process used to render it can be changed. Thus, one preservation strategy would be to maintain the original object but change the processes required to render it over time, while another would be to change the object so that it can always be rendered by current processes. The performance is defined in terms of the significant properties, or 'essence', of the object, which is what must always be preserved. It is the continued survival of these properties that determines the authenticity of the object.

Digital preservation requires the management of objects over time, using techniques that may result in frequent and profound changes to the technical representation of that record. Any preservation strategy must therefore be underpinned by a rigorous logical framework which supports the concept of multiple technical representations of an object, and the processes of change through which they arise. An example of such a framework, specifically intended for migration-based strategies, is provided by TNA's concept of 'multiple manifestations'.[4] A manifestation may be defined as: a technological instantiation of an electronic record, characterized by specific bitstream encodings, and dependent upon a specific technical environment to provide access.

The multiple manifestations model comprises the means to describe each manifestation, including its component objects, and a method for defining the 'migration pathway' used to create a new manifestation from a previous one. It therefore allows the nature, currency and derivation of each manifestation to be described, and for that description to be used as the basis for managing the manifestations within the digital repository.

In most respects, there is no significant difference between the preservation of web resources and any other digital object, and the same techniques can be applied in each case. This chapter therefore summarizes the current state of the art in digital preservation generally. It includes practical examples where possible, primarily to illustrate that the discipline has advanced considerably beyond being a purely theoretical exercise. It concludes with a discussion of its particular application to web archiving. The comparative brevity of the latter reflects the fact that little work has yet been undertaken on the specific challenges of preserving websites, a lacuna which will hopefully be addressed in the near future.

Preservation strategies

Given that preservation is concerned with preserving the means of access to a digital object, and that those means of access are subject to inevitable obsolescence, two fundamental strategies can be considered: either to develop new methods for accessing the object in its original form, or to convert the original object to a new form which can be accessed using current methods. These two basic strategies are known as emulation and migration, respectively, although variations are possible within and between these two ends of the preservation spectrum.

Emulation

Emulation strategies use software to recreate the functionality of obsolete technical environments on contemporary computer platforms. By these means, the original object can be accessed as though it were still being accessed in its original environment. Proponents of emulation strategies argue that they therefore deliver the most authentic possible rendition of the object to users. Critics point to the significant technical challenges involved in writing emulators, the difficulties of establishing whether or not the emulator itself provides a completely authentic recreation of the emulated environment, and the potential usability issues faced by future researchers when confronted by the need to interrogate obsolete interfaces. Readers are referred to Jeff Rothenberg's seminal paper for a detailed discussion of the case for emulation,[5] and to the work of the Dutch Digital Preservation Testbed Project for a comparative analysis of different emulation approaches.[6]

If one considers the network of technical dependencies discussed above, it becomes clear that a number of different approaches to emulation are possible, corresponding to emulation of different components within that network.

Software emulation

Emulation of a software package allows any object viewable by the original software to be accessed. For example, ChiWriter was a popular but now obsolete word-processing package from the late 1980s, which ran on Amstrad PCs using the CP/M operating system. No current word-processing tools can open documents in ChiWriter format. With an emulation of the ChiWriter software which runs on a modern operating system such as Windows, however, these documents can be opened and accessed by users, as though they were running the original software.

Operating system emulation

Software emulation requires the development of separate emulators for every desired software package. However, an emulator for a specific operating system could run all software which required that operating system. To return to the previous example, the development of a CP/M emulator would allow a copy of the original ChiWriter software to be installed and used to access the documents. The same emulator could also be used to run any other CP/M software. Operating system emulation therefore offers significant advantages in terms of minimizing the number of emulators that need to be developed. This may be counterbalanced by the additional complexities involved in emulating an entire operating system as opposed to a single piece of software.

Hardware emulation

Operating systems require specific hardware platforms, and the next logical step is therefore to emulate the underlying hardware. For example, contemporary PC hardware is likely to be able to support a wide variety of operating systems, including the various versions of MS-DOS, Windows, Unix and Linux. By emulating a specific hardware platform, any original supported operating system can be installed and run. This level of emulation further minimizes the number of potential emulators required, at the expense of a likely concomitant increase in the level of technical difficulty involved.

Emulating the emulator

The use of emulation creates a major technical dependency upon the emulator itself. To maintain access to the emulated objects, either the emulator itself must be preserved, or new emulators must be periodically created for the latest computer platforms.

The first approach is known as 'chaining': an emulator, E1, is written to emulate obsolete computer platform C1, running on platform C2. In time, C2 is replaced by platform C3, at which point a new emulator, E2, is written to emulate C2 on C3. E2 allows any software written to run on platform C2, including the E1 emulator, to be emulated on platform C3 (see Figure 6.2). Provided a new emulator is always written for each new platform, all previous emulators can continue to be used without modification, executing within a chain of emulators. The attraction of chaining is that it only requires a given emulator to be created once. However, the performance of chained emulators would be relatively inefficient, and that efficiency would decrease with each addition to the

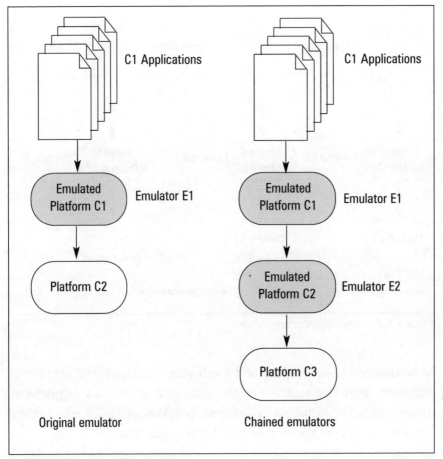

Figure 6.2   Chaining emulators

chain. It remains to be seen whether this will present a fundamental obstacle, or whether the performance degradation would be more than matched by future increases in processing power.

The alternative approach, known as 're-hosting', requires each emulator to be modified periodically to run on future platforms. Thus, in the previous example, when platform C3 replaces C2, emulator E1 would be rewritten and rehosted directly on C3. The E2 emulator would still be required, to support software written to run on C2 (see Figure 6.3). Rehosting would offer greater efficiency of performance, since every emulator will be executing directly on a given platform. However, it would require far greater resources

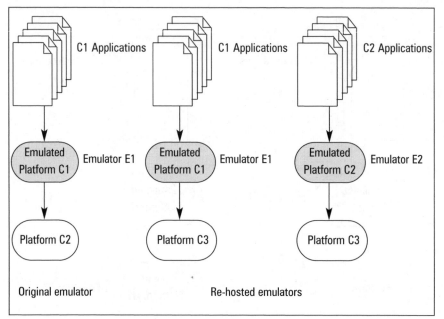

Figure 6.3   Re-hosting emulators

to be devoted to developing and modifying emulators: the number of emulators required would increase with each generation of platform, multiplied by the number of platform types. Whether such effort would be sustainable over the long term is open to question.

Virtual computers

An alternative approach to emulation is the concept of 'virtual computers'. A virtual computer creates a layer between the computer platform and the software which runs on that platform, so that the software actually executes on the virtual computer. However, unlike an emulator, which emulates a real computer environment, the virtual computer emulates something that never existed, and instead provides a standard, virtual computer platform. Software written for this virtual computer can therefore be run on any machine that supports the virtual computer. The most common example of such a virtual computer is the Java Virtual Machine (JVM), which allows software written in the Java programming language to be used on any operating system that supports JVM.

The concept of the virtual computer has led to suggestions for an Emulation Virtual Machine (EVM), which would provide a standard platform for which all emulators could be written. As each computer platform becomes obsolete, an emulator for it would be written using the EVM. At the same time, the EVM itself would be implemented on each new computer platform as it is introduced. For this approach to be successful, either the EVM itself would have to remain stable, or future versions would have to be backwards compatible. Alternatively, the chaining approach described above (see 'Emulating the Emulator') could be used.

IBM has been developing the concept of a Universal Virtual Computer (UVC), which takes this approach one step further.[7] UVC describes a very simple, flexible virtual computer, the definition of which will not change over time, thus avoiding the compatibility problems of other emulation approaches. In addition to the actual UVC, three components are required:

1   Logical data schema: This provides a conceptual blueprint for how information is structured in a particular type of object, such as a raster image.
2   UVC program: This program, which is written to run on the UVC, decodes an object in a particular format, to generate a logical data description of the object in accordance with the logical data schema.
3   Logical data viewer: This software, which is written to run on some future computer platform, renders the logical data description into a viewable representation of the object.

The archive stores the digital object itself, together with the necessary decoder and a description of the UVC and logical data schema. When the object needs to be accessed on a future computer platform, an instance of the UVC is developed for that platform, together with the necessary logical data viewer. The viewer then sends the digital object and the decoder program to the UVC, and receives the logical data description of the object back to display.

The most significant work to date on UVC has been undertaken by IBM and the Koninklijke Bibliotheek (KB) in the Netherlands. Their Long-Term

Preservation project has developed a prototype UVC implementation with decoders for JPEG and GIF images.[8] Although much work remains to be done to extend both the format coverage and support to a level that would enable UVC to be regarded as a viable preservation strategy, this remains one of the most interesting approaches to emulation.

Migration

Migration-based preservation strategies take the opposite approach to emulation, by converting the digital object, rather than the access technology, to a form accessible in a contemporary environment. The concept of converting an object from one format to another is widely understood: the 'Save as . . .' option in a software tool provides most users with their principal experience of migration. To return to the example used to illustrate emulation, a digital archivist might instead use conversion tools to migrate documents from the ChiWriter file format to one supported by contemporary software, such as Microsoft Word 2003. When the inevitable forces of obsolescence endanger the accessibility of the Word 2003 format, the documents would be converted to a future standard.

Although the principle of migration may seem straightforward, the practice can provide a significant challenge. File formats are enormously varied, and even those for specific categories of object, such as word-processed documents, display significant diversity of functionality. In part, this is a result of advances in technology, but it also reflects the efforts of software developers to establish the uniqueness of their particular products, and to retain market share by releasing new versions of products with increased sets of features on a regular basis. As a result, there is rarely a precise match between the features of the source and target formats in any migration process, which can lead to possible loss of information and functionality. Furthermore, conversion processes may themselves be imperfectly implemented, offering further opportunities for loss.

The process for migrating objects between a specific source and target format is defined by a 'migration pathway', which describes the operations required to perform the complete migration. Migration pathways can be quite complex, involving multiple steps: conversion tools to migrate directly between any two given formats may not exist, requiring the use of one or more intermediate stages. For example, no tools are available to convert ChiWriter documents directly to Microsoft Word 2003. However, a tool does exist which can convert them to the equally obsolete, but more common, WordPerfect 5.1 format. A filter for Microsoft Word is available which can convert WordPerfect documents to Word format. The migration pathway might therefore look like that illustrated in Figure 6.4.

Each stage of this process admits the possibility of information loss. There may also be a number of alternative migration pathways available. In the example, it would also be possible to convert from WordPerfect 5.1 format to WordPerfect 6.1 format, and from that to Word 2003. Each

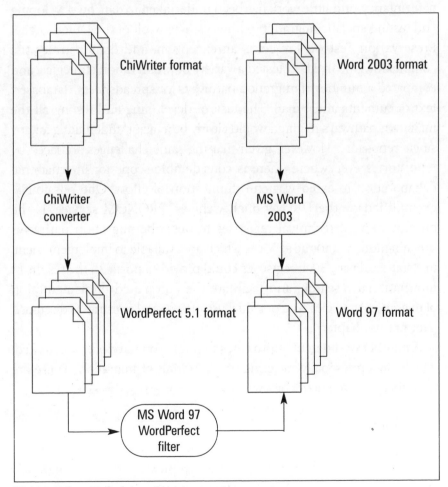

Figure 6.4   Example migration pathway

alternate pathway may yield considerably different results. Testing is therefore crucial to the successful implementation of a migration strategy. However, in order to test a migration pathway in any meaningful way, the criteria for successful migration must be fully understood. These criteria should be based on the significant properties identified for the object. The significant properties represent those aspects of the object that are deemed worthy of preservation, and the utility of a given migration pathway can therefore be defined in terms of the extent to which it successfully retains those significant properties.

The practical implementation of migration strategies is still very much in its infancy, and little work has been undertaken to date on developing and testing specific migration pathways. The work of the Dutch Digital Preservation Testbed Project is an exception, and demonstrates the complexities involved.[9] It tested a variety of preservation strategies, and compared a number of migration pathways for spreadsheets, databases, text documents and e-mail. The task of developing and testing all the migration pathways required would clearly be a major undertaking for any single repository. However, given that the same challenges are faced by repositories everywhere, there is considerable scope for international collaboration to avoid wasteful duplication of effort. One possibility, exemplified by the UK National Archives' PRONOM service, is the development of technical registries to describe migration pathways unambiguously, and the services which are available to implement them, in a standard way. Such registries could provide a portal to the results of international research, and facilitate the automated implementation of migration strategies. The potential use of technical registries is discussed later in this chapter.

A number of different approaches to migration have been advocated, which vary principally in terms of the timing of migration. These are described in more detail below.

Normalization

Normalization, which is sometimes referred to as 'migration on ingest', seeks to minimize the frequency and complexity of future migration cycles by migrating digital objects to a small number of standard formats at the point at which they are ingested into the archive. These formats will have been selected as being 'preservation-friendly', according to criteria which suggest that they are likely to have a high longevity and be simple to migrate from in future. Typically, a small range of formats will be selected, suitable for the range of different object types to be archived. Thus, one format might be selected for raster images, another for word-processed documents and a third for audio data. All objects will then be 'normalized' to this set of formats. For example, images received in a variety of formats, such as GIF, JPEG, BMP and PNG, might all be converted to TIFF.

There are several advantages to this approach. By minimizing the diversity of formats in the archive, preservation planning and the design and execution of future migration pathways are greatly simplified. In addition, the reduced number of future migration tools required may allow greater resources to be invested in each, producing a higher quality of migration. If the formats are well chosen and prove to have greater longevity than their counterparts, the frequency with which objects need to be migrated will be reduced. Finally, by selecting formats that follow open standards, and which are particularly suited to transformation, future migrations are likely to be simpler and more successful.

However, there are also potential disadvantages. Migration on ingest transfers the costs of migration to the present, when it may be argued that those costs will fall in future as techniques improve and become more efficient. Future advances in migration methods may also allow higher quality migration – a benefit which will be lost with early migration. Normalization also ties migration to the rate at which objects are being ingested into the archive, which may be relatively inefficient, and will lose the economies of scale possible through mass migration at a later date.

Normalization may be taken a stage further by encapsulating the normalized objects in a standard metadata wrapper, which enables all objects to be managed in the same way irrespective of their underlying format. An excellent example of normalization, using this approach, is provided by the National Archives of Australia. NAA have defined a set of archival formats which are deemed capable of describing the significant properties of each record type of interest. These archival formats are all defined using XML; in some cases, the format is encoded entirely in

XML but, in others, an existing binary format such as PNG is used, contained within an XML wrapper.[10] When records are transferred to NAA, they are normalized to the relevant archival format, using a specially developed software tool called Xena (XML Electronic Normalizing of Archives).[11] Both the original objects and the normalized version are then transferred to the digital repository for long-term preservation. Xena also enables the archival formats to be viewed.

It could be argued that encapsulating formats in a bespoke wrapper, access to which requires specially-written software, creates an additional and unnecessary technical dependency. The extent to which this is a genuine issue will depend upon the ability of archival institutions to maintain the supporting standards and tools which, in turn, may hinge on how widely adopted they become.

Migration at obsolescence

Migration at obsolescence lies at the opposite end of the spectrum to normalization. Sometimes known as 'just in time' migration, this approach advocates that objects only be migrated as and when dictated by technological obsolescence – that is, at the point at which they are about to become inaccessible.

The pros and cons of this approach are essentially the inverse of those for normalization. It allows each migration process to be performed en masse so that, for example, every JPEG image in the archive could be converted to PNG in a single batch process. This maximizes the efficiency and potential economies of scale achievable. Pushing the need to migrate as far into the future as possible also allows an archive to use the very latest and most advanced techniques available, which should provide the highest possible quality of migration. On the other hand, storing objects in their original formats until migration is required will create a much more diverse collection, adding significantly to the complexities of preservation planning, and possibly to the costs of management. There is also a risk that the number of tools available to migrate a given format will actually decrease as obsolescence approaches, limiting the choices available to the archivist.

Migration on demand

The strategy of migration on demand lies between these two extremes. It proposes that objects be stored in their original formats, and migrated to current formats 'on the fly' when requested by a user.

Such an approach could, potentially, offer great efficiencies, as material is only ever migrated when required. To prevent duplication of effort for popular materials, copies of each migrated object could be cached after creation. It offers the additional advantage that the user always receives a copy of the object migrated using the latest available techniques. Furthermore, the migration process can potentially be tailored specifically to the requirements of an individual user. It also offers a possible means of avoiding some of the complexities of migrating complex, interdependent objects, where migration may trigger other, sometimes unforeseen consequences: by responding dynamically to user access requests for each component, many of these interdependencies are resolved automatically.

However, this approach does add to the potential complexity of the migration process, and to the sophistication and power of the supporting infrastructure required, since this has to be performed in real time. The ability to validate each migrated object may also be compromised, which could reduce confidence in its authenticity.

An early example of this approach is being developed as part of the LOCKSS project (Lots of Copies Keeps Stuff Safe; see 'Redundancy and Backup' below). LOCKSS has implemented a prototype migration-on-demand service, based on pre-existing methods for requesting and delivering online content which are inherent to the technology of the web. The HTTP protocol allows a web browser to request a resource from a web server, and for that server to deliver the resource back to the browser. The protocol incorporates mechanisms for 'content negotiation', whereby the browser can seek to influence the choice of format, language and encoding of the requested resource. Thus, if the resource is available in multiple formats, and the browser indicates a preference in the HTTP request, the server can supply the preferred format. The browser's preferences will be based upon its capabilities to render particular formats, and therefore provide a strong measure of format obsolescence.

In practice, the majority of web resources are only available in a single format, and browser support for older formats tends to be longlasting: browsers usually therefore indicate an equal willingness to accept resources in any format. However, HTTP content negotiation offers a simple mechanism which can be used by systems such as LOCKSS to provide migration on demand. A LOCKSS server maintains a list of registered format converters. When the server receives a request for a resource, it compares the indicated format preference to the format of the original resource: if they match then the original is delivered, but if they don't, the server searches a list of registered format converters and, if an appropriate one is available, performs an 'on-the-fly' conversion to the preferred format and delivers it to the browser.[12]

The initial proof-of-concept implementation only supports conversion from GIF to PNG image formats, but illustrates the potential of such an approach.

Migration in perspective

In reality, most practical migration strategies are likely to utilize elements of all three approaches described. A strategy based on migration at obsolescence is likely to converge with normalization over time, as when particular formats need to be migrated it will clearly be desirable to normalize them to a smaller set of future formats at that point. Equally, normalization may not always be practicable, as material may be received in formats for which a normalization process has yet to be developed, and will therefore need to be archived in its original form until such time as normalization is possible. Migration on demand will be greatly simplified if the underlying, native formats have already been normalized.

The UK National Archives' preservation strategy is typical of such mixed approaches. Preferred preservation formats are selected and regularly reviewed and, where practical, objects are migrated to these formats at the point of ingest. However, in many cases this is not possible and, provided the current format is still accessible, many objects are stored 'as is', in the expectation that they will be migrated at a future date. The original manifestation of every record, in its original format, is also always archived, together with every subsequent manifestation. The practice of retaining the original bitstream, together with every successive manifestation, is becoming increasingly accepted among proponents of migration, both as a failsafe mechanism, in case later manifestations prove unsupportable and need to be recreated from earlier manifestations, and to allow for the possibility of improved preservation techniques being developed in future.

The preservation cycle

Preservation is an ongoing process: there is no end point, unless an object ceases to be considered worthy of preservation. This is equally true in the world of traditional preservation, although it may be less apparent owing to the much greater timescales between preservation interventions. The most widely adopted model for a digital archive, and for describing the place of preservation within the broader context of the operation of such an archive, is provided by the Open Archival Information Systems Reference Model (OAIS).

The OAIS model was originally developed by the space science community, and provides a generic model for the organization and management of digital archives. The model addresses the full range of archival functions, including ingest, storage, management and access, and also defines a data model for describing archival digital resources (see 'Preservation Metadata' later in this chapter). It has been ratified as an international standard (ISO 14721: 2003), and its terminology and concepts are now widely adopted. The potential of the OAIS model to serve as a benchmark for digital repositories is reflected in recent research by the UK Data Archive at Essex University, and The National Archives, to assess their compliance with the OAIS model.[13] It also forms the basis of a more wide-ranging initiative by RLG (formerly the Research Libraries Group) and the US National Archives and Records Administration to define the attributes of a digital archive, which it is hoped will lead to some form of certification scheme for trusted digital repositories (see Chapter 10, Future Trends).

However, the OAIS preservation functions have not yet been defined in detail, and the approach to preservation described here is therefore based on that developed by The National Archives in the UK (TNA). The process of digital preservation can be broken down into two fundamental areas: passive and active preservation.

Passive preservation is concerned with the maintenance of existing manifestations of digital objects. Its function is to ensure the continuing integrity of, and controlled access to, the digital objects which are contained within the preservation storage environment, together with their associated metadata. It is sometimes referred to as bit-level preservation.

Active preservation seeks to ensure the continued accessibility of digital objects over time, in the face of technological change, through active intervention. It generates new technical manifestations of objects through processes such as format migration or emulation. These new manifestations are then incorporated into the preservation storage environment for ongoing passive preservation.

These two major functions are discussed in detail in the following sections, with examples of current research.

Passive preservation

Passive preservation is concerned with the secure storage of digital objects, and the prevention of accidental or unauthorized damage or loss. As such, passive preservation needs to encompass the following functions:

• security and access control
• integrity
• storage management
• content management
• disaster recovery.

These are discussed in more detail below.

Security and access control

Any preservation storage system must provide an appropriate level of security and access control. Although the nature and degree of the controls required will vary considerably according to circumstance, the following areas will need to be addressed:

1 Physical security: The physical infrastructure required to store and
   manage the collection must be protected from accidental or deliberate
   damage. Measures may range from having locks on server room
   doors to more elaborate physical access controls, and may also include
   fire detection and suppression systems and backup power supplies.
2 System security: The IT systems must be protected from intrusions
   and malicious damage, either by external hackers and other
   unauthorized users or by malicious code or other forms of software
   attack. Typical countermeasures will include the use of password
   controls, firewalls and anti-virus software.
3 User access: The system must ensure that users have appropriate access
   rights to the stored content. For example, in the case of archival
   material it is likely that few, if any, users will be authorized to alter or
   delete stored objects. Additional access controls will be required if the
   content of the collection is in any way sensitive: in the case of web
   archives, some content may not be publicly accessible for legal reasons.
4 System access: Human users are not the only possible agents that need
   to be controlled: software systems can access and change data. The
   storage system must therefore ensure that software access to the
   archive is appropriately controlled. This includes preventing malicious
   code, such as viruses and worms, from executing.

Integrity

The integrity of a digital object arises from the assurance that it has not
been altered in any unauthorized manner. Possible threats to the integrity
of an object include accidental corruption, deliberate alteration by an
unauthorized user, and alteration caused by malicious code, such as a virus.
These threats can be controlled in part using the security and access
measures described in the previous section. However, it remains essential
to test the integrity of the archival collection periodically: preservation of
integrity is the fundamental goal of passive preservation, and integrity
checking therefore provides the ultimate assurance that this function is
being successfully performed. Integrity checking will be required for
both the data and the associated metadata.

The standard method for testing that a bitstream has not been altered at the bit level is to calculate some form of digest. A digest (often referred to as a checksum) is a value which is based on the content of the bitstream, calculated using some form of mathematical algorithm. The digest algorithm is designed so that a change of a single bit will result in a completely different digest value. If a digest value is calculated for a file at the point of ingest into the storage system, then the integrity of that file can be tested at any future date by recalculating the digest and comparing it to the original value: any difference will demonstrate that the file has been altered in some way. Commonly used digest algorithms include MD5[14] and SHA-1.[15]

The recorded digest values are, of course, themselves vulnerable to deliberate or accidental alteration. It is therefore strongly recommended that they be managed separately from the object storage system.

A potential issue with the use of digests arises from the possibility of 'collisions', whereby two different bitstreams can produce the same digest. All digest algorithms allow for this as a theoretical possibility, but the degree of real danger varies. In some cases, these collisions are purely random, and the chances of an altered file yielding the same digest as its unaltered state are vanishingly small. However, in others it has proved possible to deliberately alter a file and yet retain the same digest value. The strength of particular digest algorithms is constantly changing, but is an important factor to consider when selecting one. The extent to which this is an issue will depend upon the type of threat being protected against: if the main danger is accidental corruption then a weaker algorithm may be perfectly adequate, whereas in situations where there is a genuine risk of deliberate alteration, a much stronger algorithm may be required.

The frequency with which the integrity of each stored object should be checked will also need to be determined. This should be based upon an assessment of the risks to that integrity. For example, an appropriate frequency for checking media corruption should be based upon the estimated failure rate of that medium.[16]

Storage management

Storage management is concerned with the physical storage of the collection and, in particular, the medium on which it is recorded.

Media selection

Digital information is physically manifested as bytes encoded on some form of storage medium, such as a hard disk, a magnetic tape or a DVD. All such information is vulnerable to loss resulting from either natural deterioration of, or artificial damage to, the medium. A variety of fundamentally different storage technologies currently exist, each with its own unique mechanisms for decay and susceptibilities to damage. Current technologies can be broadly subdivided into magnetic and optical types.

Magnetic-based storage media use the polarity of magnetic particles to encode information, such that one polarity corresponds to a binary 'one', and the other to a 'zero'. These particles can be supported on a variety of base layers, the most common being flexible tapes and rigid hard disks. A wide variety of (generally incompatible) magnetic tape technologies exist, driven by a very competitive market for high-capacity offline storage.

Optical technologies utilize materials that can be made to reflect laser light in different ways to achieve their effect, principally through the use of dyes or physical pits in the surface of the medium. The most common types of optical storage are varieties of compact disc (CD) and digital versatile disc (DVD). In both cases, the recordable and rewritable versions of these technologies have followed a similar pattern of development, whereby the initial emergence of competing and incompatible standards has been followed by gradual convergence on a single standard.

Storage technologies are subject to very rapid change, in response to the ever-increasing demand for higher-capacity storage at lower cost. In addition to the development of higher-capacity hard disks, magnetic tapes and optical disks, a number of entirely new technologies are likely to appear in the near future. These may include holographic storage and the widespread adoption of high-capacity Flash-based storage (see Chapter 10, Future Trends).

No computer storage medium can be considered archival, irrespective of its physical longevity – technological obsolescence is inevitable. The need to refresh electronic records periodically onto new media is inescapable for the foreseeable future. Nevertheless, careful selection of appropriate media can maximize the periods between refreshment cycles and simplify the refreshment process, in addition to providing the most secure storage environment possible.

The following criteria should be considered when selecting archival storage media:

1   Longevity: The medium should have a proven life span appropriate to its intended use and the planned refreshment cycle. Great longevity (e.g. more than ten years) is not necessarily an advantage, as obsolescence of drive technology often precedes physical deterioration of the storage medium.

2   Capacity: The medium should provide a storage capacity appropriate for the quantity of data to be stored and the physical size of the storage facilities available. Minimizing the number of actual media to be managed will usually create efficiencies and resource savings.

3   Viability: The media and drives should support robust error-detection methods for both reading and writing data. Provision for testing the integrity of media after writing is also a benefit. Proven data recovery techniques should also be available in case of data loss. Removable media should be write-once, or have a reliable write-protect mechanism, to prevent accidental erasure and maintain the evidential integrity of the data.

4   Obsolescence: The media and their supporting hardware and software should preferably be based on mature technology, rather than leading-edge technology, and should be well established in the marketplace and widely available. Media technologies which are based upon open standards for both media and drives should generally be preferred to those which are proprietary to a single manufacturer.

5   Cost: Two elements must be considered when assessing the relative costs of storage media – the cost of the media and the total cost of ownership. Valid comparisons of media costs must always be made on a price per gigabyte basis. The total cost of ownership will include costs for purchasing and maintaining the necessary hardware and

software, and of any storage equipment required. Support costs and the quoted mean time before failure of both the drive and the media must also be taken into account.

6   Susceptibility: The media should have a low susceptibility to physical damage, and be tolerant of a wide range of environmental conditions without data loss. Magnetic media should have a high coercivity value (preferably in excess of 1000 Oersteds), to minimize the chances of accidental erasure.[17] Any measures required to counter known susceptibilities (such as packaging or storage requirements) should be affordable and achievable.

Evaluating media

Specific media types can be evaluated against these criteria to identify those most appropriate to a particular organization's needs. The evaluation process should fully take into account variations within a media type. For example, a number of different dye and metal layer combinations are available for CD-Rs, which offer varying degrees of longevity. A sample methodology for conducting such evaluations is provided in TNA's guidance on the selection of removable media.[18]

In situations where multiple copies of data are stored on separate media, it may be advantageous to use different media types for each copy, preferably using different base technologies (e.g. magnetic and optical). This reduces the overall technology dependence of the stored data. Where the same type of medium is used for multiple copies, different brands or batches may be used in each case, to minimize the risks of data loss due to problems with specific manufacturers or batches.

Media refreshment

Storage technologies are subject to the same forces of technological change and subsequent obsolescence as every other part of the network upon which access depends. The actual media themselves also have widely varying life spans. Although claims of considerable longevity have been made for certain media types, these are essentially irrelevant to the issue of preservation. Given that the technology required to access the media will become obsolete over relatively short timescales, the maximum longevity required for any archival storage medium is no greater than that of the supporting technology: the fact that a given type of medium will still be theoretically readable 100 years from now will be of little comfort to future curators faced with the fact that the drive necessary to read the information has been obsolete for 80 of those years.

Approaches that advocate the transfer of digital information to non-digital storage media, such as microfilm, are also unsustainable. The option to output a human-readable rendering of a digital object, such as an image of a page of word-processed text, is only applicable to a very narrow range of material: no such option exists for an interactive 3D model or a database, for example. The alternative, of outputting the underlying binary data itself, introduces more problems than it solves. Not only does it introduce a new technical dependency – the requirement to be able to transfer the information back into a machine-processable format to allow access – it also fails to address the issue that the majority of the network of technical dependencies is still required: the same combinations of hardware and software will still be necessary to render the information into human-readable form.

The relatively transient nature of digital storage media is, however, counterbalanced by the fact that the very nature of digital information allows multiple, identical physical instances, and that the ability to produce perfect copies allows the number of physical instances to be increased as required. In the digital realm, the concepts of 'an original' and 'a copy' have no meaning – all copies of a digital object are created equal. There is no analogue to this in traditional media – a paper manuscript has a single physical manifestation and, although copies can be made, they will inevitably be inferior to the original, since some information will always be lost in the copying process. It is, however, common to maintain digital information perfectly in multiple instances, and on multiple media types, over time.

Digital objects therefore have to be preserved in digital form, using digital storage media, and accepting that, although the information itself can be preserved, the physical media on which that information is stored will change over time. The challenge is therefore to manage the inevitable process of change, and this is achieved through the technique of media refreshment. A long-established and widely practised process, refreshment entails the periodic transfer of digital information from one storage medium to another instance of the same type, or to an instance of a different type. Which of these alternatives is required at a given point will depend upon the relationship between the longevity of the medium and that of its supporting technology, which has already been discussed. For example, magnetic tapes which are being accessed on a very frequent basis are likely to have a relatively short life span, and their content may well need to be regularly refreshed onto new copies of the same tape type. On the other hand, it may prove that information stored on CD-R and rarely accessed may not require refreshment until the actual technology is superseded, at which point it will be refreshed onto an entirely new media type.

In either scenario, the techniques are the same. The information must be physically copied between the two media, using the appropriate drive technology for each, and the copying process must be verified, to ensure that the information has been copied without corruption or loss. Techniques for performing such verification are common, and generally involve the use of checksums (see 'Integrity' above). Given the inevitable increases in storage capacity that come with new generations of media, it is likely that any programme to refresh to new types of media will result in a reduction of the number of physical media instances required, and hence a rationalization of the physical content of the media. The storage management system in use will need to be updated to reflect this.

Redundancy and backup

The fact that digital objects can be copied perfectly, with each copy having equal authority, can be utilized to great advantage for passive preservation. Having multiple copies of an object minimizes the risk of loss or damage, and can also provide an important safeguard against technological obsolescence. The concept of multiply-redundant copies is therefore a cornerstone of digital preservation. The number of copies necessary to provide appropriate redundancy is debatable, and also likely to be dictated by the needs and available resources of a particular organization. However, three copies, at least one of which is stored at a separate geographical location, should be regarded as the minimum.

In some scenarios, it may be possible to utilize much higher levels of redundancy. The LOCKSS (Lots Of Copies Keeps Stuff Safe) project is an excellent example of this.[19] LOCKSS is open-source software developed to provide libraries with a simple and inexpensive way to preserve and deliver the content of e-journals over the web. The system provides a highly distributed network of preservation appliances – PCs which collect, store and distribute the content. Copies of the content are stored on multiple appliances, and the system continually compares the copies to detect errors. Having such a distributed system avoids the need for individual appliances to be backed up. However, such an approach may not be appropriate in all cases – for example where security is a particular issue.

The redundant copies must be managed, to ensure that the various copies remain synchronized and to resolve any discrepancies that might arise. Backup is one method by which redundant copies may be created, and involves the periodic copying of data to another medium. This will typically be to a removable medium such as magnetic tape.

Content management

The stored collection does not exist in a vacuum – it must be possible to add new content, export copies of content, update content (such as metadata) and even, in exceptional circumstances, delete content. The preservation storage system must therefore provide facilities for digital objects and their associated metadata to be added, copied, amended and deleted within the store, subject to the appropriate security and access controls.

Disaster recovery

An archive is a valuable, possibly unique, resource, and it must therefore be appropriately safeguarded from both natural and manmade disasters. This requires that some form of disaster recovery plan be in place, which describes how an operational archive service will be restored in the event of a major incident disrupting or preventing that service. The disaster recovery plan will need to address the restoration of both the content of the archive, and the technical and operational infrastructure required to support it. The plan will therefore need to include the following:

- detailed instructions for staff to follow in the event of different types and scales of disaster scenario
- contact details for key staff and emergency services, including specialist disaster recovery contractors
- instructions for restoring the collection content from backup copies
- a complete description of the hardware and software infrastructure, sufficient to allow procurement of replacement components as required
- copies of all software required to operate the systems
- copies of crucial documentation, such as operating procedures and manuals.

Testing the disaster recovery plan is every bit as important as developing it. An untested plan cannot be assumed to be workable, and testing will not only allow staff to rehearse their response but will also undoubtedly reveal flaws or overlooked issues in the plan. A full-scale disaster recovery drill can be a major and time-consuming exercise, and it may only be possible to do this on an occasional basis. However, individual elements of the plan can and should be tested regularly. It is also essential to remember that systems and circumstances change, and the plan must be kept up to date to reflect this.

Practical tools for passive preservation

Although most of the functions of passive preservation can be implemented individually, for anything other than the smallest collection specialized digital repository software is the only practical solution. Fortunately, a growing number of such systems are now available, many of them under open-source licences. These tend to fall into two categories:

1   Mass storage systems: Mass storage systems provide standard interfaces to heterogeneous storage systems, such as robotic tape libraries and hard disk arrays, which may be located at several physical locations.

They allow the virtualization of multiple storage systems, so that they can be treated as a single storage device. Such interfaces are essential to managing very large data collections. Examples include the Storage Resource Broker, developed by the San Diego Supercomputer Centre, and CASTOR, developed by CERN.

2   Repository systems: Repository systems are concerned with the management of digital objects, typically providing functionality for ingest, retrieval, version control, cataloguing and searching. Many systems have been designed for the digital library community, to provide academic institutions with the means to manage electronic scholarly publications, such as e-prints. Examples include DSpace, developed by Massachusetts Institute of Technology and Hewlett-Packard, Fedora, jointly developed by the University of Virginia Library and Cornell University, EPrints, developed by Southampton University, and LOCKSS, developed by Stanford University and previously described.[20]

These digital repository systems vary in the extent to which they provide the full range of passive preservation functionality, and none yet offers any significant provision for active preservation. However, it is actually desirable that the two should be separated. A single system which attempted to provide all preservation functionality would almost certainly be too large and complex to develop or maintain, and modularity is an important design consideration for systems that will be required to have lengthy life spans: it allows individual components to be replaced as technology dictates, without having an adverse impact on other elements of the overall system. However, a digital repository must support active preservation, allowing access to its content via the appropriate active preservation functions.

Active preservation

Active preservation generates new technical manifestations of objects through processes such as format migration or emulation, to ensure their continued accessibility within changing technological environments. It comprises three basic functions, operating in a continuous cycle, potentially supported by the services of a technical registry (see Figure 6.5).

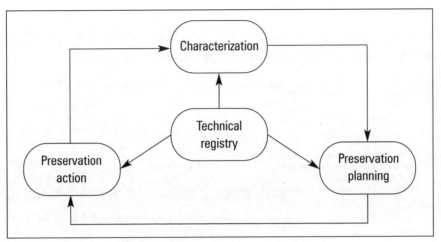

Figure 6.5   The active preservation cycle

These are discussed in the following sections.

Technical registries

A registry is an information source that provides a common reference point for a particular community of users. By registering key information concepts, the community can benefit from a shared understanding of what those concepts mean: in effect, it provides a common vocabulary. In the case of a technical registry for digital reservation, these concepts relate to the technical dependencies of digital objects. The most commonly cited example is the file format registry. Without an agreed standard for describing the formats of objects, there is enormous potential for ambiguity: for example, if one object is described as being in JPEG format, and another is described as being in JFIF 1.02 format, how can we tell if this is actually the same format? A file format registry, containing standard definitions of each format, provides a solution: if everyone describes formats with reference to the registry definition then all ambiguity is removed. A standard referencing mechanism can be provided if each registry record is also assigned a persistent, unique identifier.

However, not only file formats benefit from registries: their use can potentially be extended to every element of the representation network, including character encoding schemes, compression algorithms, software, operating systems, hardware and storage media. PRONOM, the first such operational registry, was developed by The National Archives of the UK (TNA) in 2003, and is available as a free online resource (see Figure 6.6).[21]

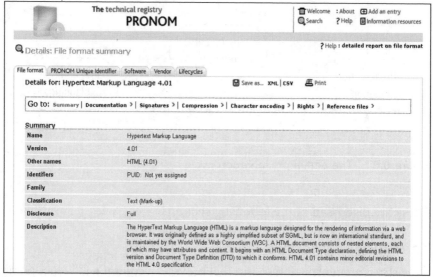

Figure 6.6   The PRONOM registry (The National Archives)

The 2005 version of PRONOM (PRONOM 4) provides a searchable database of technical information about file formats, software tools, operating systems and other technical components. It also offers an extensible scheme of PRONOM Unique Identifiers (PUIDs), which provides persistent, unique and unambiguous identifiers for file formats.[22] Adoption of the PUID scheme is growing: for example, it is the recommended encoding scheme for describing file formats in the UK's e-Government Metadata Standard.[23] In future, the scheme may be extended to include other technical components described by PRONOM, such as operating systems and compression algorithms.

Although PRONOM is available as an international resource, the provision of all required technical registry services is almost certainly beyond the resources of any one organization. This has led to the concept of a distributed global network of such registries, with each node in that network developing and sharing content. Proposals for a project to develop a Global Digital Format Registry are currently being formulated,[24] and PRONOM is likely to become one of the first nodes in the planned network.

Examples of how technical registries can support long-term preservation are discussed in more detail in subsequent sections.

Characterization

Before any object can be preserved, it must be understood with sufficient technical precision. Specifically, it is necessary to understand the significant properties of the object, which must be preserved over time if it is to be regarded as authentic, and its technical characteristics, which will influence the specific preservation strategies which may be employed. To give a very simple example, the resolution and colour depth of a raster image are likely to be considered fundamental properties to preserve. Equally, the fact that it is stored in TIFF version 6.0 format, using CCITT T.6 image compression, will constrain the available preservation options.

Characterization comprises three discrete stages: identification, validation and property extraction.

Identification

This determines the precise format and version of the object. This is a fundamental element of characterization information, and enables the subsequent selection of format-specific characterization tools to perform other characterization processes. Identification is typically performed using some form of signature, a digital 'fingerprint' which is unique to a specific format. The simplest such signature is provided by a file extension, but this has the major disadvantages that it is often not unique to a single format version and can easily be altered. The most reliable identification can be achieved using internal signatures – particular sequences of binary values within a file which are common to all files of a specific format.

The DROID (Digital Record Object IDentification) software developed by TNA is an example of an identification tool that uses both internal and external signatures to perform automated batch identification of file formats.[25] DROID is also significant as an example of a preservation tool which uses a technical registry: the signatures used by DROID are stored in the PRONOM registry, with updates being automatically downloaded to the tool over the web.

Validation

This determines whether the object is well formed and valid against its formal specification. It is a relatively mechanistic process, provided that the specification is available, and validation tools have been developed for a range of format types. Examples include a number of commercial PDF validators, the W3C's online HTML and XHTML validation service,[26] and the JHOVE software developed by Harvard University,[27] which can identify, validate and extract metadata for a growing number of formats. Repositories will need to record both the results of validation and objects for which validation is not currently possible, to enable future validation as new tools appear.

Property extraction

This measures those properties of the object which are significant to its long-term preservation. These can be divided into two categories:

1 Representation characteristics: These are characteristics deriving from the particular technical manifestation of an object, which define the technical dependencies upon which access depends, and therefore determine the available preservation options. These will include both explicit characteristics, such as the file format specification to which the object conforms, character encoding schemes and compression algorithms employed, and implicit characteristics, such as the technical environment required to render the object, including hardware, software and operating system dependencies.

2 Inherent characteristics: These are characteristics deriving from the underlying nature of the object itself, rather than any specific technical manifestation, and constitute the properties that must be preserved over time, and across multiple technical manifestations, in order to maintain the authenticity of the object. These may relate to the form of the object (e.g. the resolution of a raster image, the sample rate of

an audio recording or the fonts used in a document) or to its content (e.g. the date on which an e-mail was received).

In both cases, these properties may be explicitly or implicitly identifiable, and may be derivable either from the object itself or from an external source. For example, the compression algorithm employed in a raster image may be identified by a specific value within the object bitstream, or may be established by default through identification of the file format. Equally, an XML document may require an external schema to allow certain properties to be determined. These properties may also be subdivided into generic and specific properties. The generic properties of the object format can be predetermined and recorded in a technical registry, and therefore do not need to be separately measured for each object instance. However, the properties specific to a singular object must be measured for each instance.

Tools for property extraction are available for many formats. These range from commercial software to tools developed specifically for preservation purposes. The latter include the previously mentioned JHOVE software, and the metadata extractor developed by the National Library of New Zealand.[28]

Preservation planning

Preservation planning forms the decision-making heart of active preservation. Its role is to identify and monitor technological changes and their potential impacts on stored digital objects, and to develop the necessary detailed preservation plans to mitigate against those impacts. The approach to preservation planning developed by TNA, which is designed to be universally applicable, comprises four distinct processes: risk assessment, technology watch, impact assessment and preservation plan generation.

Risk assessment

Every object is subject to a risk assessment at the point of ingest. This risk assessment is based upon a set of standard criteria, selected as key indicators of the current risks posed to the continuing accessibility of the object. These criteria can be divided into generic and specific risk factors. Generic risk factors are common to all objects in a given format, such as the degree of public disclosure of the format specification or the current diversity of software support, and can be directly calculated by reference to information stored in a technical registry. Specific risk factors are those that relate to a single instance of an object, such as the presence of macros in a Word document or the use of external fonts in a PDF file. These can be identified using characterization tools. The result of the risk assessment is used to determine the urgency of preservation action: a low risk may simply indicate that the risk assessment should be recalculated at a future date, whereas a high risk will trigger immediate action.

Technology watch

'Technology watch' describes the process of continually monitoring technological change, which can be manifested as updates to the content of a technical registry. These updates may change the risk criteria described above. For example, the cessation of support for a particular software product might alter the risk associated with formats supported by that software. Owing to the complex interdependencies that exist between technical components, changes to registry content can have significant follow-on impacts on other, related content.

Impact assessment

This process analyses the results of risk assessments and technology watch, to determine their actual impact upon the objects stored in the repository. For example, a change to a risk criterion caused by technology watch will require new risk assessments to be undertaken on all affected objects. Equally, objects which were previously assessed as low risk need to be periodically reassessed: the impact assessment function determines when this is the case, and identifies the affected objects.

Preservation plan generation

The final stage of preservation planning is to determine the detailed preservation action required. This takes the form of a preservation plan, describing the precise technical processes to be undertaken. Alternative possible plans may be identified. Each will then need to be rigorously tested to determine whether or not they meet the defined authenticity criteria. Once an appropriate plan has been approved, it must be documented in sufficient detail to allow its subsequent execution.

As an example, a preservation plan might take the form of a migration pathway, which details the steps necessary to migrate an object from one technical manifestation to another. A migration pathway can therefore be defined in terms of a sequence of migration tools, together with any necessary configuration parameters. Information about migration tools can be recorded in a technical registry, enabling migration pathways to be defined with specific reference to the registry. In addition, information about the formats that particular software can render and create forms the basis for identifying potential migration pathways.

Current approaches to preservation planning

A number of projects are beginning to develop risk assessment techniques for digital objects. The Online Computer Library Center's INFORM project has developed a methodology for quantifying the risk factors affecting digital formats and measuring their potential impact on preservation decisions.[29] The PANIC project, at the University of Queensland's Distributed Systems Technology Centre, is developing a semi-automated preservation service for scientific data, which will allow monitoring of archival collections, support decision-making about preservation actions and then invoke the appropriate preservation service (such as a format conversion service), using the Semantic Web (see Chapter 10, Future Trends) and web services.[30] Cornell University's Virtual Remote Control project, described in Chapter 3, Selection, is developing risk assessment and remote monitoring services which are specifically aimed at web-based content,[31] and build on previous seminal work in this field.[32]

An important avenue of investigation has been opened up by research being undertaken at the Vienna University of Technology, into the application of utility analysis to preservation planning. Utility analysis is a technique for objectively describing and evaluating alternative strategies, and appears to offer strong potential for preservation planning.[33] As part of the DELOS Network of Excellence, it is currently being integrated with the Dutch Digital Preservation Testbed, described earlier in this chapter.

Preservation planning can utilize the services of technical registries such as PRONOM. Information used to assess risks for specific criteria, such as the product support lifecycles of the technologies required to create or render electronic records, which are a significant factor for determining obsolescence, can be recorded in the registry. Technology watch can then be viewed as the process by which that registry information is maintained and updated: changes to that information trigger re-evaluation of the relevant risk criteria and updating of the associated risk assessments. The registry can also assist in the generation of preservation plans: in the case of TNA, which uses a migration strategy, migration pathways can be identified by analysing information about the formats that a particular software tool can read and write.

Preservation action

Preservation action represents the enactment of the preservation plan, in accordance with the chosen preservation strategy. Typically, this will entail either the migration of objects to new formats or the development of emulated environments. In the case of migration, this will almost certainly be performed as an automated process, whereby the selected migration pathway is executed without further human intervention. It is also likely to be undertaken as a batch process, involving the migration of many objects at once.

Whatever preservation plan is adopted, preservation action requires the availability of specialized software tools. In some cases, existing tools may be re-used for preservation purposes: for example, there is a plethora of tools for converting between many different file formats. However, it is inevitable that other tools will need to be developed for the specific needs of digital preservation. As has been previously described, such tools are increasingly being developed within the library and archival community. In many cases, they are made freely available for others to use, often under open-source licences that allow others to contribute to their continued development. Such collaborative approaches will be essential to the development of a comprehensive and practical preservation toolset. However, it will be increasingly important for curators to engage with the commercial sector, which develops the vast majority of the hardware, software and operating systems used to create the resources we need to preserve. Widespread, practical digital preservation will only be achieved when long-term access is universally recognized as a key requirement of their customers, and suppliers respond by developing products in which sustainability is a fundamental feature.

The preservation action stage cannot be considered complete until the results have been validated, to ensure that the planned action has been completed successfully. In this context, the criterion for success will be that the preserved object remains authentic, according to whatever authenticity criteria have been previously defined. Validation therefore requires that the significant properties of the preserved object (i.e. its performance) be measured and compared with the benchmark provided by the equivalent performance of the original object. This is achieved through the characterization process, thereby completing the preservation cycle.

The principle can be illustrated through the example of how a basic object migration might be validated. The significant properties of a raster image are likely to be comparatively simple. For the purposes of this example they might comprise:

- the horizontal and vertical dimensions of the image in pixels
- the resolution in dots per inch (dpi)
- the colour depth in bits per pixel
- the colour space (e.g. RGB or CMYK)
- the image histogram, which measure the distribution of colour values within the image.

Characterization could be used to measure these properties for an original image in GIF format. After the image has been migrated to a new format, such as PNG, the same properties can be measured for the new image. If the properties are equal, within defined tolerances, then the migrated image can be considered valid in terms of the defined authenticity criteria.

Images provide a very simple example, and the potential problems of defining comprehensive significant properties for more complex types of material should not be understated. However, it seems unarguable that digital archivists must undertake such an endeavour: if one cannot define concrete metrics by which successful preservation can be assessed, then preservation is impossible.

Preservation metadata

The maintenance of detailed descriptive information, or metadata, is a fundamental requirement for the proper management of digital resources. The broader issue of catalogue metadata has already been described in Chapter 5, Quality Assurance and Cataloguing. However, the specific needs of long-term preservation require additional technical metadata. This preservation metadata is necessary to support both passive and active preservation processes. The most detailed model of the types of preservation metadata required is provided by the OAIS Reference Model (see 'The Preservation Cycle' above), which defines the following categories:

- Preservation description information: This includes the information required to preserve the object's content adequately over time. It includes information about the referencing, context, provenance and fixity of the object.
- Packaging information: This describes how a digital object is physically stored on some form of storage medium.
- Descriptive information: This describes the content of the digital object, for the purposes of resource discovery and access by users.
- Representation information: This describes how an object can be represented in a meaningful form. The need to provide information on how the representation information should itself be interpreted can require the maintenance of complex representation networks. Representation information is subdivided into structure information, which describes structural rules and concepts that apply to the object, and semantic information, which gives meaning to the structure information.

The OAIS model does not provide any form of detailed metadata scheme. However, the recent work of the PREMIS working group has taken this next step, defining a specific set of preservation metadata elements.[34] It is too early to know whether the PREMIS Data Dictionary will receive widespread adoption, but it currently the closest thing to an international standard available.

It is possible to generate the majority of preservation metadata automatically, for example through processes such as characterization as described above.

Preservation metadata provides the means to understand and interpret a digital object. This creates a fundamental dependency between those objects and their metadata, which must be maintained over time. Preserving the link between an object and its metadata record is therefore an essential requirement of long-term preservation. Current thinking is divided on the best means of ensuring this. The metadata can be used to encapsulate the object, creating a single new object which contains both. This certainly creates the closest physical binding between the two, but does impose an additional barrier to accessing the underlying object, and can create extremely large objects to manage. The alternative is to use identifiers to link the objects to metadata stored elsewhere, for example in a database. This does create a less direct link, but proponents would argue that techniques for doing so are sufficiently mature and reliable as to present no serious risk. Whichever approach is adopted, the maintenance of the preservation metadata and its relationship to the objects it describes is a fundamental prerequisite of digital preservation.

Preserving web resources

Although the preservation of web resources requires the same fundamental approach as any other form of digital preservation, it does occupy a position towards the upper end of any scale of complexity, and therefore highlights a number of specific issues worthy of further exploration.

Preserving complex objects

A website is, by definition, a complex object. It comprises a hierarchy of interconnected objects: a website is composed of many individual web pages, and each page itself has many components, such as HTML and images. These components are related in multiple ways. The hypertext link is perhaps the most obvious of these, but other types of relationship may also be significant. For example, in a static website objects will be organized into a folder structure, which imposes an order on them. This folder structure may be intimately connected to the hypertext relationships, if relative path names are used. Preserving a website therefore entails not only preservation of the individual components, but also preservation of the relationships between them, which allow the whole to be recreated from the sum of its parts.

Any method for preserving complex objects must achieve two fundamental goals. First, it must provide some means of describing the relationships between the components of the object and, second, it must ensure that any preservation actions that result in a change to one component are reflected by updating all the related components. The first of these goals is the more straightforward. Websites are, essentially, self-describing in terms of their structure: for example, hypertext links are encoded within the web pages themselves. Nevertheless, other organizational relationships, such as the underlying folder structure, will need to be described within the metadata description of the website.

The second goal is more complex to achieve, as can be illustrated through example. A simple website might contain HTML pages that include images stored in GIF format. The relationships between the HTML pages and their associated images are described in the <img> tags in the pages. A decision might be made to migrate the GIF images to a new format, such as PNG. Once the images have been successfully migrated, each <img> reference in the relevant web pages will need to be updated to point to the migrated image instead of the GIF original. Thus, a preservation action on one component object can have knock-on effects upon other objects, and the relevant relationships must therefore be understood if that preservation action is to be successfully completed.

Preserving behaviour

Objects that allow some form of dynamic interaction with users are said to exhibit behaviour, and this may be considered a significant property to preserve. However, by its very nature, behaviour presents a major preservation challenge. Unlike static properties, such as the dimensions of an image, behaviour arises out of the interaction between user and system, and will vary depending on the user's decisions and even, potentially, who the user is. Two fundamental approaches to capturing this may be possible. First, the rules that govern the behaviour could be preserved, allowing the same behaviour to be recreated using different technologies. This could be described as 'input-based' behaviour preservation. Second, the range of possible behaviours could be captured as transactions between the user and the system – 'output-based' behaviour preservation. In both cases, the complexity increases in step with the complexity of the rule system. The input-based approach might be achieved through emulation, or by using a technology-neutral method for encoding rule systems. The output-based method might involve capturing each transaction as a static representation.

By definition, any website exhibits behaviour, since at the very least it processes requests from a user and delivers web resources in return. More complex behaviours can be introduced through the use of scripting languages such as JavaScript, embedding dynamic content such as Flash within web pages or using database-driven websites. Preserving the simplest behaviours of a static website is relatively straightforward, using the input-based approach, as the relevant rules are encoded within the HTML of the web pages (e.g. hypertext links), and HTML is an open standard. The possibility of capturing transactions as static objects has already been discussed in Chapter 4, Collection Methods, and would support output-based preservation. However, much work remains to be done to develop proven techniques for preserving complex behaviour.

Conclusion

Digital preservation represents a formidable challenge, at both a technical and an organizational level. Many of the issues can only be resolved through collaboration, and will require a sustained global effort. However, this should not be seen as grounds for pessimism: every element of the preservation process described in this chapter has a potential or actual solution, and the discipline is rapidly advancing in breadth, depth and sophistication. In many cases, the major challenge now is to draw the diverse threads into a cohesive solution. This is dependent more upon organizational will, at all levels, than on technology, and the imperative for curators to continue to lobby on behalf of the preservation agenda has never been greater.

Notes and references

1   Garrett, J. and Waters, D. (eds) (1996) *Preserving Digital Information: report of the Task Force on Archiving of Digital Information*, Commission on Preservation and Access and The Research Libraries Group, www.rlg.org/legacy/ftpd/pub/archtf/final-report.pdf [accessed 19 February 2006].

2   Adobe Systems Incorporated (1992) *TIFF Revision 6.0*, http://partners.adobe.com/public/developer/en/tiff/TIFF6.pdf [accessed 28 October 2005].

3   Heslop, H., Davis, S. and Wilson, A. (2002) *An Approach to the Preservation of Digital Records*, National Archives of Australia, www.naa.gov.au/recordkeeping/er/digital_preservation/green_Paper.pdf [accessed 28 October 2005].

4   Brown, A. Multiple Manifestations: managing change in a digital preservation environment, *Digital Preservation Technical Paper*, **3**, forthcoming, London, The National Archives.

5   Rothenberg, J. (1999) *Avoiding Technological Quicksand: finding a viable technical foundation for digital preservation. A report to the Council on Library and Information Resources*, Council on Library and Information Resources, www.clir.org/pubs/abstract/pub77.html [accessed 28 October 2005].

6   Slats, J. (ed.) (2003) *Digital Preservation Testbed White Paper: emulation: context and current status*, ICTU, www.digitaleduurzaamheid.nl/bibliotheek/docs/white_paper_emulatie_en.pdf [accessed 31 October 2005].

7   Lorie, R. A. (2002) The UVC: a method for preserving digital documents – proof of concept, *IBM/KB Long-term Preservation Study Report Series*, IBM Global Services.

8   See Appendix 1 for more information about the KB's UVC prototype.

9   See www.digitaleduurzaamheid.nl/ [accessed 19 February 2006] for further information.

10   Details of the currently defined XML formats are available at www.naa.gov.
     au/recordkeeping/preservation/digital/xml_data_formats.html [accessed
     19 February 2006].

11   See Appendix 1 for more information about Xena.

12   Rosenthal, D. S. H., Lipkis, T., Robertson, T. S. and Morabito, S. (2005)
     Transparent Format Migration of Preserved Web Content, *D-Lib
     Magazine*, **11** (1),
     www.dlib.org/dlib/january05/rosenthal/01rosenthal.html [accessed 28
     October 2005].

13   Beedham, H., Missen, J., Palmer, M. and Ruusalepp, R. (2005) *Assessment
     of UKDA and TNA Compliance with OAIS and METS Standards*, UK Data
     Archive, University of Essex, www.data-
     archive.ac.uk/news/publications/oaismets.pdf [accessed 18 February
     2006].

14   Rivest, R. (1992) *RFC 1321: the MD5 message-digest algorithm*, Internet
     Engineering Task Force, www.ietf.org/rfc/rfc1321.txt [accessed 18
     February 2006].

15   Eastlake, D. (2001) *RFC 3171: US secure hash algorithm (SHA-1)*, Internet
     Engineering Task Force, www.ietf.org/rfc/rfc3174.txt [accessed 18
     February 2006].

16   An example of how this might be calculated is provided in RLG (2005)
     An Audit Checklist for the Certification of Trusted Digital Repositories, RLG
     and National Archives and Records Administration,
     www.rlg.org/en/pdfs/rlgnara-repositorieschecklist.pdf [accessed 23
     October 2005].

17   Coercivity is a measure of the amount of magnetic field required to reduce
     magnetic induction to zero, i.e. erase the medium.

18   Brown, A. (2003) Selecting Storage Media for Long-term Preservation,
     Digital Preservation Guidance Note, **2**, London, The National Archives,
     www.nationalarchives.gov.uk/preservation/advice/pdf/selecting_
     storage_media.pdf [accessed 23 October 2005].

19   See http://lockss.stanford.edu/index.html [accessed 19 February 2006].

20   See Appendix 1 for more information about SRB, CASTOR, DSpace,
     Fedora, and EPrints.

21   See www.nationalarchives.gov.uk/pronom/ [accessed 19 February 2006].

22 Brown, A. (2005) The PRONOM PUID Scheme: a scheme of persistent unique identifiers for representation information, *Digital Preservation Technical Paper*, **2**, London, The National Archives, www.nationalarchives.gov.uk/aboutapps/pronom/pdf/pronom_unique_identifier_scheme.pdf [accessed 19 February 2006].

23 See www.govtalk.gov.uk/schemasstandards/metadata_document.asp?docnum=872 [accessed 19 February 2006].

24 See http://hul.harvard.edu/gdfr/ [accessed 19 February 2006] for further information.

25 See Appendix 1 for more information about DROID.

26 See Appendix 1 for more information about the W3C validator.

27 See Appendix 1 for more information about JHOVE.

28 See Appendix 1 for more information about the NLNZ metadata extractor.

29 Stanescu, A. (2004) Assessing the Durability of Formats in a Digital Preservation Environment: the INFORM methodology, *D-Lib Magazine*, **10** (11), www.dlib.org/dlib/november04/stanescu/11stanescu.html [accessed 19 February 2006].

30 See http://metadata.net/newmedia/ [accessed 19 February 2006] for further information about PANIC.

31 See http://irisresearch.library.cornell.edu/vrc/ [accessed 19 February 2006] for further information about VRC.

32 Lawrence, G. W., Kehoe, W. R., Rieger, O. Y., Walters, W. H., and Kenney, A. R. (2000) *Risk Management of Digital Information: a file format investigation*, Council on Library and Information Resources, www.clir.org/pubs/abstract/pub93abst.html [accessed 28 October 2005].

33 Rauch, C. and Rauber, A. (2004) *Towards an Analytical Evaluation of Preservation Strategies: presentation for the ERPANET workshop, 10-11 May 2004, Vienna*, Technische Universität Wien, www.erpanet.org/events/2004/vienna/presentations/erpatrainingvienna_rauber.pdf [accessed 28 October 2005].

34 PREMIS Working Group (2005) *Data Dictionary for Preservation Metadata: Final Report of the PREMIS Working Group*, RLG and Online Computer Library Center (OCLC), www.oclc.org/research/projects/pmwg/premis-final.pdf [accessed 19 February 2006].

Chapter 7
Delivery to users

Introduction

Any web archive requires some mechanism for allowing its designated community of users to access its content. This is true even if the only users are staff in the collecting organization. Such a delivery system needs to provide two basic functions: a means for users to discover content of interest and a means to deliver that content to the user in a meaningful form.

That meaningful form derives from two aspects of the archived content:

1 Context: The original and current context of the archived content should be clearly indicated. This includes maintaining the integrity of the relationships between various elements of archived content, describing the provenance of that content, and providing a clear distinction between the archived content and any 'live' instances of that content which may also be extant.

2 Authenticity: The archived content should be delivered in a form which is authentic to the original, subject to the particular authenticity requirements of the collecting organization. Any divergence between the archived content and the original, such as missing content or functionality, should be highlighted.

Each of these can pose significant challenges, many of which are unique to the delivery of archived web content. It must also be emphasized that, to date, relatively little research has been undertaken into the potential use of web archives, and our understanding of the types of usage that will need to be supported by delivery systems is therefore immature. This chapter provides an overview of how both functions may be provided, and of the issues that can arise when providing access to archived web content.

Search and browse access

The two fundamental methods used to discover and navigate web content are searching and browsing. Searching is the most common method for initially finding content of interest, while a degree of browsing is likely once an initial starting point has been identified. Structured, browseable methods for finding content can also be useful for users with particular or pre-existing knowledge. For a web archive delivery system to be genuinely useful, it must therefore support both modes to some degree.

Search access

Search access provides a vital tool for users. A number of options are available. At a minimum, it should be possible to search for content on the basis of some form of title or URL. However, the most powerful option is provided by full-text searching across the entire collection content. Modern web search engines are capable of sophisticated searching within the most common types of textual content found on the web, including HTML and XML web pages, PDF files and word-processed documents. These search engines can be just as easily deployed to search a web archive.

Browse access

Providing browse access typically involves the categorizing of content into some predetermined hierarchy through which users can 'drill down'. Thus, websites could be arranged according to some form of subject classification, with increasing levels of granularity. This type of access can be very useful in certain cases, but only if the chosen classification scheme matches the expectations of the user. However, web archives will typically have many different groups of users, often with widely differing requirements. For example, an archive of health-related websites which is aimed primarily at medical professionals might be organized according to a scientific typology of conditions and treatments. However, to a layperson, such an arrangement might be extremely confusing and essentially unusable.

Such hierarchies also tend to impose a single view on the collection, although more sophisticated approaches, which support multiple alternative hierarchies, are also possible. Nonetheless, the user's options for browsing are always limited by the classification decisions made by the archive.

The creation of browse access also requires the manual assignment of all content to particular classifications, which can be resource-intensive. For these reasons, it is generally better to keep such browse access to a comparatively simple level.

The development of an appropriate classification system for browsing may be additionally complicated within a consortium scenario (see Chapter 9, Managing a Web Archiving Programme), where the delivery system may be required to support access to the collections of several partner organizations, which may have different cataloguing traditions. For example, the UK Web Archiving Consortium (UKWAC) needed to develop a classification scheme that met the needs of both libraries and archives. However, although this made decision-making more complex, it did help to ensure that the resultant scheme was simple to use.

Case study

Our Digital Island, a web archive developed by the State Library of Tasmania, provides a good example of a relatively simple search and browse interface (see Figure 7.1 overleaf).[1] Users can browse via a multi-level subject hierarchy, or through alphabetical subject or title indices, or can perform searches across the catalogue metadata.

Catalogue entries for individual website snapshots are displayed with thumbnail images (see Figure 7.2 overleaf). The level of catalogue information provided is high compared to many web archives, and includes information about technical dependencies and loss of functionality (see 'Functionality' below).

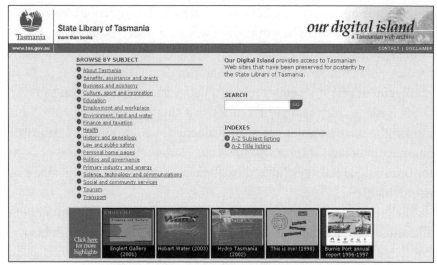

Figure 7.1   Our Digital Island – browsing (State Library of Tasmania)

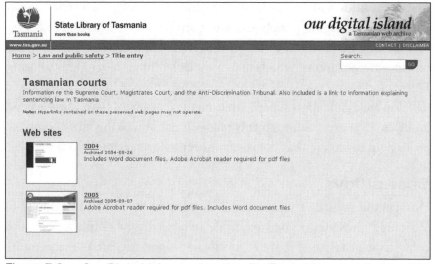

Figure 7.2   Our Digital Island – thumbnails (State Library of Tasmania)

External search engines

Search engines play a fundamental role in the behaviour of web users, and an understanding of this is essential to the development of a successful delivery system. Failure to take account of this is an all-too-common trap for the unwary, and may have a detrimental effect on both the user's experience and usage of the live website.

Considerable efforts can be devoted to the construction of an elaborate front-end to a collection, without considering that many users will bypass this using external search engines. The first point for consideration must therefore be the extent to which the collection content is exposed to search engines: if every instance of a website is open to indexing by search engines, then these instances will appear within the search engine's search results, and users will be able to navigate directly to them, bypassing the majority of the delivery system.

It is also essential to be aware of the impact of search engine indexing on the live versions of archived websites: it is entirely possible that search engine hits for archived versions will outnumber and outrank those for the live website. This is clearly undesirable both for users, who may be unaware that they are viewing an obsolete version, and who may actually be seeking the current version, and for the website owners, who may suffer a commensurate loss of users.

The simplest means to constrain the behaviour of search engines is to use a 'robot exclusion notice' (see 'Crawl Settings' in Chapter 4, Collection Methods). This is a standard file, placed on a web server, which contains a set of rules defining the extent to which automated agents, such as search engine crawlers, may access the content of the website. By defining appropriate rules in its robots.txt file, a web archive delivery system can limit search engine access to particular parts of the system, such as high-level catalogue records.

Placing archived content in context

Every element of content in a web archive has multi-dimensional relationships with other internal and external content. These dimensions may be categorized as structural and temporal, and each plays a part in defining the context of that content.

A website is composed of multiple individual elements of content, and the relative relationships between these must clearly be maintained in order to retain a functioning website. However, a website is also likely to contain relationships to external content, which may or may not be captured at the point of archiving. These relationships form the structural context of the website.

Although it is these structural relationships that predominate in a live website, in a web archive every structural relationship also has a temporal aspect. Collecting activities take place over time, and may be repeated. Thus, multiple instances of a website may co-exist within the same collection, if the archiving body is collecting the site on a periodic basis, or may be spread across multiple collections if the site falls within the collecting policy of more than one archiving body. These instances are differentiated on the basis of the time of collection.

Any relationship between two items of archived content, such as a hyperlink, is therefore defined in terms of both structure and time, and consistency must be maintained on both levels if the archive is to be meaningful. For example, the homepage of a website might contain an image which is changed every week. If multiple instances of that web page have been archived, then each must retain the association to the correct image for the moment of collection. Equally, if two websites are regularly collected, and one contains an external link to the other, that link should always point to the corresponding instance of the second website.

However, the temporal dimension is not entirely straightforward. Although collection methods such as direct transfer can be considered to produce a true 'point-in-time' snapshot of a website, where every element can be considered to have been collected at precisely the same moment, techniques such as remote harvesting collect a site over a period of time. For a large site, this process might take several days. As a result, different components of the site will have slightly different temporal contexts. Unless the site is highly dynamic, and has experienced significant change during the collection period, this is unlikely to present a problem. However, this may create a genuine issue in the relationships between discrete websites, which may be separated more widely in time. This raises the following question: how large a variation in collection time is too great to allow two sites to be considered contemporaneous?

There is no simple answer to this question, and it must be left as a matter for individual organizational policy. However, the ability to distinguish clearly between various instances of archived content on the basis of structural and temporal relationships is certainly a fundamental requirement of any delivery system.

The local context

The delivery system must manage the context of web content stored within the local collection. Examples of how this can be achieved are described in 'Delivery Methods' below.

The global context

Using available access tools, it is straightforward to provide simple and clear navigation for users within a discrete archival collection. However, given the growing number of web archives, and the limitations on how much content a single archive can collect, there are clear advantages to providing links between collections. For example, a user browsing a website in the Internet Archive's web archive might follow a link to content which has not been archived by the Internet Archive. At present, that user is simply presented with a message to this effect, and it is left to their own ingenuity to discover whether that content has been captured in some other archive. However, with tools and standards available to support interoperability between archives, it is conceivable that the response to a user clicking an unarchived link would be to initiate an automatic search across other archives for that content. If found, the content could then be seamlessly delivered to the user. The potential of an interoperable network of web archives is huge, and would allow the creation of a virtual global archive. Although this potential has yet to be realized, some small steps have been taken in this direction. For example, the UKWAC archive provides seamless access across content collected by multiple organizations, albeit within the same physical collection.

The 'live' context

One key difference between web archiving and traditional collecting is the distinction between the 'live' and 'archival' environments. Web content can be collected very rapidly and, by its very nature, leaves the source content unaffected. It is a process of replication, rather than transfer, whereby a new, archival copy is created which must co-exist with, rather than replace, the original. Although that period of co-existence will be temporary (otherwise there would be no requirement for archiving), it may still be of significant duration. As a result, the relationship between the live version and the archival copy must be managed. This is essential to prevent any user confusion about which copy is being accessed. It is clearly undesirable for a user to view a live website while under the impression that they are viewing an archived version; there are equally obvious reasons why the reverse situation could be disastrous.

A web archive must therefore take steps to ensure that all archive content is clearly signposted to users. This can be achieved in a number of ways, including:

- a standard statement to users, similar to that discussed for describing changes in functionality (see 'Functionality' below)
- through the URL, as in the case of the Wayback Machine, where all archived resources are clearly identified through the standard URL prefix (see 'Functionality' below); the disadvantage of this method is that it may not be immediately obvious to the user
- a standard message which is automatically displayed whenever the user selects a link that will take them to content outside the archive.

These approaches can be used in combination to offer the greatest clarity. However, it should be noted that they only address the potential for confusion in a user who is browsing the collection. Archives must also be aware of the risks that can arise from the use of search engines. These are discussed in 'External Search Engines' above.

From the opposite perspective, if the relationship between the archiving organization and the website owner is appropriate, then it may be mutually beneficial for the website owner to indicate the availability of archived versions on the live website. For the archiving body, this provides an alternative access point to the collection, and may generate additional usage; for the website owner it can provide a simple alternative to providing continued access to non-current content. For example, TNA provides an 'Archived by The National Archives' logo, which can be used by webmasters

Figure 7.3
TNA 'Archived by' logo
(The National Archives)

(see Figure 7.3). The logo can be directly linked to the appropriate section of the UK Government Web Archive.

Delivery methods
Static web content

For static web content which has been collected by remote harvesting or direct transfer, delivery requires 're-hosting' of the content. Re-hosting involves making the content available in the same manner as any other website – by placing that content on a web server and making it accessible to users. The only prerequisite for this is that the structural integrity of the website be intact, in other words that all the necessary components are present, in the correct structure, and that all links are relative rather than absolute. If this is the case then the archived website should be displayed correctly. The deliverable functionality will be determined by the re-hosting environment. For example, any original search facility will only function if it is either replicated on the new host, or replaced by a new, generic search capability.

The following case studies describe two operational delivery systems for static content.

Case study: the Wayback Machine

The Wayback Machine provides an interface (Figure 7.4 overleaf) which allows users to locate archived website snapshots, to differentiate between multiple snapshots of the same site collected on different dates and to navigate across all content collected at a certain point in time, effectively recreating the original context of that content. Users search for specific content within the archive using its original URL. All archived instances of that URL can be viewed on an index page, which displays them in date order. The index also distinguishes between instances that contain changed content by the addition of a '*' beside the date of the snapshot.

In a Wayback Machine archive, all hypertext links are preserved in their original form. The Wayback Machine dynamically rewrites those links to

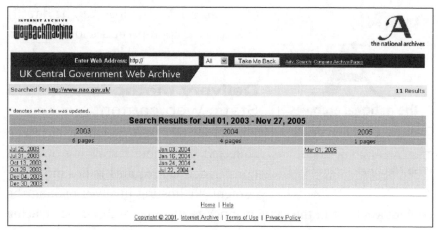

Figure 7.4   The Wayback Machine (The National Archives)

refer to their new context within the archive every time they are accessed. An original link can be converted to its archived equivalent by the simple addition of a prefix in the form [URL of archive collection]/[date of snapshot]/[original URL]. The snapshot date can be replaced by a wildcard character that will match any date. Thus, for example, if an archived page contains a link to 'http://www.mysite.com/', this might be rewritten as 'http://www.archive.org/mycollection/20051006/http://www.mysite.com/'. The rewritten link would therefore point to the version of 'www.mysite.com' archived within the collection on 6 October 2005. If there is no snapshot of the linked content available in the archive that matches the precise date, the Wayback Machine will retrieve the closest matching date. If the linked content has not been archived then an appropriate message is displayed. In this way, the Wayback Machine allows archived content to be navigated and viewed in its original context, while minimizing the need for archival intervention in the original content. However, the dynamic link rewriting process does have limitations. For example, links that are generated using JavaScript, or contained within binary objects such as Flash-driven menus, cannot be rewritten and thus will continue to link to the live version of the website. This can potentially create confusion between the archival and the live context of resources (see 'The "Live" Context' above). At present, the Wayback Machine does not support full text searching – users can only search for content by URL.

Case study: WERA

The IIPC's WERA tool takes a broadly similar approach to the Wayback Machine. WERA comprises an Access module, which requires two additional components:

- a search engine to provide a full text search facility; the NutchWAX search engine is currently supported (see Appendix 1)
- a Document Retriever module which provides the interface between WERA and the actual web archive; a Document Retriever module for accessing content stored in ARC format is provided with WERA,[2] but modules to interface with other types of collection could also be developed.

The WERA interface allows a user to search in two ways:

- by URL, if the URL of the desired content is known
- by full text searching across the collection.

Searches can also be restricted to specific date ranges. In each case, search results are displayed in a standard form (see Figure 7.5 overleaf). An individual result can be viewed in one of two ways:

1   The 'timeline' view displays the archived content (see Figure 7.6 overleaf). At the top of the page, the WERA interface displays information about the snapshot version being viewed, and allows the user to perform further searches. It also shows the chronological context of the snapshot through a graphical timeline, which allows the user to navigate easily between different snapshots of the same content. The user can choose the resolution of this timeline (e.g. in months or years).

2   The 'overview' mode displays an index of the available snapshots, in a similar manner to the Wayback Machine. Selecting a snapshot causes it to be displayed in the timeline view. WERA dynamically rewrites links to point to archived content in a similar manner to the Wayback Machine.

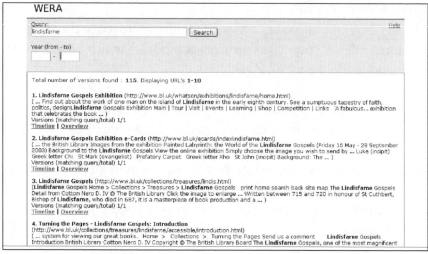

Figure 7.5   WERA search results (National Library of Norway)

Figure 7.6   WERA timeline view (National Library of Norway)

A demonstration installation of WERA has been set up by the IIPC, and can be viewed online.[3]

Dynamic web content

The options for delivering dynamic web content will be constrained by the method of collection used. Content which has been remotely harvested

– in effect transforming it into a static representation – can be delivered using the methods for harvested content described in the previous section. If a site has been collected by direct transfer, then re-hosting is an option: this will potentially allow the site to be accessed in its original, dynamic form.

However, the increasing availability of tools specifically designed for archiving deep web sites, such as DeepArc (see Chapter 4, Collection Methods), does allow another possibility. These tools extract the content of a database into a standard, open format such as XML. Generic access tools can then be used to recreate the original functionality of the website. An example of this approach is the Xinq (XML Inquire) tool developed by the National Library of Australia, and released as part of the IIPC Toolkit.[4] This is designed to provide access to XML databases, such as those generated using DeepArc. Xinq enables a curator to create search and browse functionality which corresponds to that provided by the original website. There are, of course, limitations on the extent to which original behaviour can be recreated – the new interface will be a reinterpretation, rather than a facsimile, of the original. However, this approach has obvious advantages over either static representation or re-hosting. First, it enables dynamic behaviour to be recreated, which is simply not achievable with a static version. Second, it only requires the archive to support a single access interface, rather than attempting to maintain a plethora of different dynamic web technologies for multiple re-hosted sites.

Figure 7.7 overleaf illustrates the use of DeepArc and Xinq to provide archival access to a dynamic website, the Health Education Remote Rural Resources Database (HERRD). The underlying database content has been captured and transformed to XML using DeepArc. A new interface has then been created with Xinq. Although there are significant presentational differences from the original, the essential functionality has been preserved.

Supporting data mining

Web archives are not purely of interest to users seeking specific archived web content: there is a growing body of research into the structure and behaviour of the web, which may make increasing use of web archives.

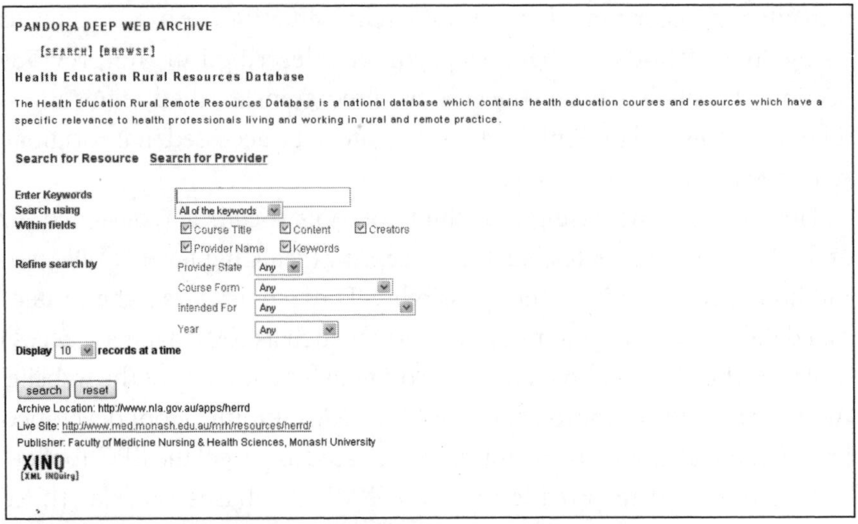

PANDORA DEEP WEB ARCHIVE

[SEARCH] [BROWSE]

Health Education Rural Resources Database

The Health Education Rural Remote Resources Database is a national database which contains health education courses and resources which have a specific relevance to health professionals living and working in rural and remote practice.

Search for Resource   Search for Provider

Enter Keywords
Search using   All of the keywords
Within fields   ☑ Course Title   ☑ Content   ☑ Creators
                          ☑ Provider Name   ☑ Keywords
Refine search by   Provider State   Any
                          Course Form   Any
                          Intended For   Any
                          Year   Any
Display 10 records at a time

[search] [reset]
Archive Location: http://www.nla.gov.au/apps/herrd
Live Site: http://www.med.monash.edu.au/mrh/resources/herrd/
Publisher: Faculty of Medicine Nursing & Health Sciences, Monash University

XINQ
[XML INQuiry]

Figure 7.7   Xinq version of HERRD website (National Library of Australia)

Approaches such as hyperlink network analysis and webometrics draw on the standard techniques of social network analysis and citation analysis, respectively, to investigate the formation and persistence of hyperlinks within the web environment, and the information they can provide about social interaction and communication between online users. Although most studies have been based on the 'live' web, the potential value of web archives is also beginning to be recognized.[5] For some time, the Internet Archive has provided tools to support these forms of data mining, as an alternative to using the Wayback Machine to access its collections, and other web archives may be expected to support similar demands in future.

Supporting citation

As with any form of archival collection, a web archive needs to support persistent citation. In other words, users will require a permanent method for referencing archived content. This will be particularly essential for academic users of web archives, who may be citing such content in published works.

To support this, the web archive will need to ensure that all content is assigned a unique reference, which will not change over time and will be persistent. The obvious reference to cite for web content is a URL. However, in this case the archive will need to take steps to ensure that the URLs for its collection are persistent. This requires either that the URLs will not change or, if they do change, that this is made invisible to users through some form of resolution system, whereby the citable URL is automatically translated into the current internal URL in the collection.

An example of the use of persistent URLs is provided by the Australian Pandora web archive. This assigns persistent identifiers to websites in accordance with the scheme developed by the National Library of Australia.[6]

Access control

If it is necessary to restrict access to some, or all, of the content of a web archive then some form of access control will have to be provided. This may require users to register and log on before they can view content.

In some circumstances, it may be necessary to restrict the uses to which archived content can be put. In many cases, the terms and conditions of use may require the source of reused archive content to be acknowledged. It may also be possible to enforce this through some form of digital rights management (DRM), which places physical restrictions on the uses of content, such as for copying or printing. However, DRM protection mechanisms tend to be specific to certain types of content (e.g. PDF documents), and a generic solution may be difficult to achieve.

Functionality

The functionality of an archived website may differ from its live counterpart for two fundamental reasons: that functionality cannot be captured or preserved, or that the archive has deliberately disabled that functionality.

Lost functionality

Certain types of functionality may be impossible to capture with a given collection method. For example, search functions cannot be preserved through remote harvesting. Where such losses are a known feature of the chosen collection method, or are detected as part of quality assurance, this should be indicated to users in some way .

Disabled functionality

It may be necessary for an archive to disable certain functionality deliberately, in order to maintain the integrity of the archived website or prevent inappropriate behaviour. For example:

1   Visitor counters: Many websites include an automatically incremented display of the number of visits received. It is desirable that this counter be frozen at the visitor count current at the time of archiving, or removed altogether, rather than continuing to function.

2   System date and time: Many web pages display the current system date and time for the web server. For the archived version, it is desirable that this display be frozen at the point of archiving, or removed altogether, rather than continuing to function.

3   External links: A website is very likely to contain hypertext links which point to resources not present in the archive. Since these resources are beyond the control of the archive, and their continued existence cannot be guaranteed, the functionality of such links will almost certainly decrease over time. Rather than allowing users to be confronted by a 'page not found' error, or become confused about whether or not they are currently viewing content within or outside the archive, it is desirable that such links be managed in a consistent way. They may be disabled entirely, or simply redirected to a standard web page which explains that the link may no longer exist, and optionally allows the user to proceed. Advertising pop-ups should be treated in a similar manner.

4   E-mail links: Many websites contain e-mail links and it is essential that all such links be disabled on the archived site.

Highlighting lost or disabled functionality

All deliberately disabled functionality should be indicated to users. Two possible approaches to this are:

1   A standard statement displayed to users:
    —   immediately before they access the site, which explains the types of functionality that have been disabled; this is the simplest

method and can be effective where certain kinds of functionality have been universally disabled across a collection

— as a standard banner on the homepage of the archived site, or even on every page.

2   Individual markers to highlight each instance of disabled content. For example, all e-mail links could be replaced with a standard message detailing the nature of the function that has been disabled. The advantage of this method is that it highlights the intervention in context – users may not remember a generic statement displayed prior to access. The obvious disadvantages are that such interventions will alter the appearance of the web page and may affect the formatting of subsequent content, and extra work will be required to insert these placeholders (although much of this could be automated).

Case study

The user interface developed by TNA for its UK Government Web Archive provides an example of a simple delivery mechanism that offers facilities for both searching and browsing. Behind the scenes, the delivery system is divided into two parts: initial access is provided through a search and browse system developed by TNA and hosted on its own web servers, but access to the individual websites' snapshots is provided via a Wayback Machine interface hosted on the servers of the European Archive. This division is essentially transparent to users.

The provision of a search system was considered essential, given that the original search facilities of the individual archived websites could not be replicated. In the first instance, a 'URL search' was provided using existing functionality already available through the Wayback Machine. This allows users to search the collection for a specific URL, which might be the homepage of a website or the URL of any component of that website. Although a useful tool for users who already know what they are looking for, this offers no help to the user who is interested in any material in the collection on a given subject. For this reason, a full-text search facility has subsequently been developed. This search engine can index the textual content of web pages, PDF files and Microsoft Word documents, and therefore exposes the vast majority of textual material within the archive to search-based access. This enhanced search engine, which offers an interface similar to standard web search engines such as Google, is being implemented by TNA in 2006.

Users can also access the collection by browsing through categories of related websites. TNA's web archive, being based on a thematic selection policy, lends itself to this approach. The interface provides a top-level set of categories corresponding to the themes of the selection policy, such as 'Defence and Foreign Policy' and 'Health and Education'. Upon selecting a category, the user is presented with a list of the available websites within this category. Selecting a website takes the user to the Wayback Machine index page for that site, which lists the available snapshots. In this way, users can easily drill down from broad subject areas to specific website snapshots.

Conclusion

Delivery systems can vary considerably, depending on the types of content they contain and the user communities they serve. However, every delivery system must be focused primarily on the needs of its users, in terms of both how it allows them to discover content of interest, and how it presents that content to them. It must respect the local and global context of the content within the collection, and its relationship to the original 'live' environment. It must also maintain the content's authenticity, and clearly signpost any changes or lost functionality. Perhaps most importantly, a delivery system must be designed to accommodate its user community's preferred methods of access, including appropriate mechanisms for searching, browsing, analysing, reusing and citing archived resources.

Notes and references

1   See http://odi.statelibrary.tas.gov.au/ [accessed 19 February 2006].
2   The ARC format is described in more detail in Chapter 2, The Development of Web Archiving.
3   See http://nwa.nb.no/wera/ [accessed 19 February 2006].
4   See Appendix 1 for further information about Xinq.
5   Thelwall, M., Vaughan, L. and Björneborn, L. (2005) Webometrics, *Annual Review of Information Science and Technology*, **39**, 81–135.

6 See www.nla.gov.au/initiatives/persistence.html [accessed 19 February 2006] for further information on the NLA's persistent identifier scheme.

Chapter 8
Legal issues

Introduction

It is unsurprising that a medium such as the web, which combines global impact and accessibility with the facility for very intimate and individual interaction, raises a plethora of complex legal issues. It is equally predictable that the archiving of web content would therefore be subject to similar legal complexities. Legislation may affect many aspects of web archiving, including the collection of content, its preservation, and the dissemination of that content to users.

First, the moral rights of individuals or organizations may be affected, most notably rights to privacy and rights over the protection of intellectual property. These rights may potentially be infringed by a number of web archiving activities, including collection, preservation and delivery. Human rights must also be considered, especially in the context of disseminating potentially distressing or offensive material.

Second, tensions may exist between the requirements of the selection policy and the governing legal framework. For example, it may be necessary to collect material that contravenes libel or obscenity laws. This may have a fundamental impact on the processes of collection, and especially on delivery.

Finally, a collecting organization may well be constrained or driven by its own legislative requirements, or those governing its potential content suppliers. This may include archival or legal deposit legislation, freedom of information legislation, or the demands of regulatory compliance or public accountability.

The legal situation is further complicated by the fact that the web is multi-jurisdictional: a web archiving programme may well be collecting content from sources, and very likely delivering that content to users, in many different countries governed by a wide variety of legislative frameworks.

Any organization planning to implement a web archiving programme must therefore be aware of all relevant legal requirements, and consider their potential impact on that programme. It is beyond the scope of this book to provide a detailed analysis of the specific national and international legislative requirements that may be relevant. Rather, this chapter provides a brief overview of the major issues to be considered, together with suggested sources of more detailed advice. It concentrates on examples from UK legislation, with reference to other regimes where appropriate. It should be noted that, although the categories of legislation discussed are common to many countries, and similar issues can therefore be expected to arise in each case, the precise framing of specific national legislation can vary in subtle ways, which can have significant ramifications. It is therefore essential that the legal requirements of the relevant jurisdiction are fully understood.

As might be expected in a new and rapidly evolving discipline, many of the potential legal issues affecting web archiving have yet to be tested in the courts, and are therefore subject to a degree of uncertainty.

It is strongly recommended that any organization considering the establishment of a web archiving programme should, as a minimum, assess whether or not these activities may be subject to any specific legal requirements and, if there is any likelihood that this is the case, seek legal opinion.

Intellectual property rights

The most common types of intellectual property rights are copyright, which concerns rights in created 'works', and patents, which govern rights to inventions. From the perspective of archiving websites, the most significant issue arises from intellectual property rights, and especially copyright, which may apply to collected material. The content of a website will almost certainly qualify for some form of copyright protection and, in order to avoid breaching that protection, the collecting body must:

- identify the owners of any intellectual property rights invested in the material being collected
- ensure that those rights are not infringed by any action undertaken by the collecting body.

Other issues may arise from the need to perform certain kinds of preservation action, such as migration, which alter the form of protected content.

Copyright

A website is not, in itself, protected by copyright, although it may well be subject to database rights (see below). However, its content almost certainly will be subject to copyright. As such, the acts of copying, altering or disseminating web content require the permission of the appropriate copyright owner. Since web archiving will almost certainly involve all three of these actions, great care must be taken to ensure that no copyright infringement results from them.

Database right

The World International Property Organization (WIPO) adopted a Copyright Treaty in 1996, to address new issues raised by the information society. Its provisions include the protection of computer programs as literary works, and additional protection of databases. It also prohibits the circumvention of rights protection technologies and the unauthorized modification of rights management information. Within the European Union, the Treaty was implemented in EU Directives 91/250/EC, 96/9/EC and 2001/29/EC, while the Digital Millennium Copyright Act 1998 (DMCA) served the same purpose in the United States. The specific concept of database right, covered by EU Directive 96/9/EC, was introduced into UK law through the Copyright and Rights in Databases Regulations 1997. Database right alters and extends existing copyright protection for databases. In this context, a database is defined as a systematic arrangement of independent materials which are accessible by electronic or other means. Although the range of materials that may be included within this definition is somewhat ambiguous, it is likely that a website would be considered a database. Database right applies specifically to the act of collecting, verifying, arranging and presenting the database content. The actual content of the database, the intellectual design of the database structure and any software used to implement the database may all be subject to their own copyright. Database right restricts the extraction or reuse of the database content on a similar basis to copyright.

Copyright and preservation

To maintain the long-term accessibility of a digital object, that object may have to be transformed in some way, for example by migrating it to a new format (see Chapter 6, Preservation). Preservation will also certainly require the creation of bit-perfect copies of those objects. Copyright law is typically formulated in the context of traditional forms of created work, in which there is a meaningful distinction between the original and a copy. Such concepts are essentially obsolete for works which are 'born digital', and the application of copyright legislation in such cases can therefore be ambiguous. Although it is clear that the creation of an exact copy of a digital object would fall within the definition of copying for the purposes of copyright, it is less certain whether more interventionist measures, such as migration, should be considered to be copying or adaptation.

In the UK, the Copyright, Designs and Patents Act 1988, as amended by the Copyright (Librarians and Archivists) (Copying of Copyright Material) Regulations 1989, makes provision for prescribed libraries and archives to make copies of material for preservation purposes. However, while this may well cover acts of passive preservation, it seems likely that procedures such as migration would be considered to be an adaptation, for which no special dispensation is available.

Digital objects may also be protected by rights protection mechanisms – technologies designed to prevent unauthorized copying or use. These mechanisms are proprietary and technology-specific, and will therefore become obsolete over time. Long-term preservation may therefore require the circumvention of such mechanisms in order to maintain access to the content. However, the circumvention of such mechanisms is itself an infringement of copyright under the WIPO Treaty and subsequent national laws. Although in the UK there is a right of appeal to the Secretary of State where such devices prevent the owners of copies from exercising their legitimate rights, this remains an area of ambiguity for digital preservation.

Alternatives to copyright

In recent years there has been increasing debate about the appropriate balance between the rights of creators and those of users. This has led to the proposal of alternative models, by which authors can assign much greater freedom of use on a universal basis. An author's right to copyright protection of their work is enshrined in law and cannot be removed. These alternatives, which are often referred to as 'copyleft', must therefore work within the existing legal framework. They typically provide mechanisms whereby the author assigns a perpetual licence to every user of their work to use, modify, copy and distribute derivatives of that work without restriction. 'Strong' copyleft licences additionally require that all derived works inherit the same copyleft licence as the original, whereas under 'weak' copyleft some derivatives may not be so protected.

Examples of copyleft licences include the GNU Free Documentation License,[1] and certain of the Creative Commons licences.[2] Copyleft licensing is being used for a wide variety of web content, and may work to facilitate web archiving. In this context, metadata standards have also been developed to facilitate the automatic identification of web content which is thus licensed. However, it should be noted that any copyleft licence must articulate correctly with the specific copyright legislation of the appropriate jurisdiction: for example, a licence written to conform to US law may not be enforceable under other jurisdictions.

Patents

Patents are intellectual property rights in an invented device, method or substance. Although patents are unlikely to have any direct impact on web archiving, other than the possible implications of patented web technologies for long-term preservation, it is interesting to note that web archives are playing an increasingly important role in the determination of prior art. The granting of a patent requires that the subject of the proposed patent be novel – that is, not previously described in a publicly accessible form. This is usually determined through a prior art search. Given the pervasiveness of the web as a publication method, it is unsurprising that web publication has become an increasingly important consideration in establishing or contesting prior art, and that web archives are therefore emerging as an important reference source in such cases.

Approaches to managing rights issues

A number of possible approaches to managing the issue of intellectual property rights within a web archiving programme are possible. The three most commonly adopted are:

1   Explicit permission: Many web archives obtain the explicit permission of the copyright owner before collecting any material, in order to obtain an appropriate licence to collect, preserve and make available that material. This approach is certainly the most resource-intensive, and can place severe limitations on the volume of material that can be collected. For example, the Netarkivet.dk project in Denmark, which harvested web content related to county and district elections in 2001, found that the cost of negotiating permissions completely dominated the overall project costs.[3] However, it also reduced the risk of possible infringement to a minimal level. The UK Web Archiving Consortium has adopted this approach; the licence agreement developed by UKWAC may serve as a model, and is reproduced in Appendix 2.

2   Legislative mandate: Certain collecting bodies may enjoy specific freedoms with regard to copyright. For example, in the UK the Public Records Act 1958 (see below) makes specific provision for The

National Archives (TNA) to collect material which is declared a public record, and to make copies of those records available to users on request, without infringing copyright and irrespective of any permissions or prohibitions set by the copyright owner. This provision extends to any website which is a public record. It should be noted that these freedoms do not, of themselves, permit the redistribution by TNA of those materials via the internet, which is classed as 'communicating to the public'. However, the majority of public records are Crown Copyright: TNA has the right to redistribute such records on the web, both by virtue of its status as a government department and under the waiver of Crown Copyright for public records.

3   Retrospective take-down: Some web archives do not seek explicit copyright permissions for the material they collect, but instead operate a policy that they will remove any infringing material from the archive upon notification by the copyright owner. The most notable exponent of this approach is the Internet Archive. However, it must be emphasized that such a policy offers no protection under copyright law, and exposes the archive to potential litigation.

Ultimately, any web archive must take a risk management approach to these issues. Specifically, it must assess the risks that:

1   It will collect or disseminate material and, by so doing, infringe copyright.
2   A copyright owner will seek legal redress in the event of infringement.
3   The archive will be held liable in the event of litigation.

A proper assessment of these risks should allow an appropriate approach to be identified. For more detailed guidance on the issue of copyright in an archival context, the reader is referred to more specialist works.[4]

Privacy

Privacy legislation governs the management of personal information relating to individuals, and is intended to protect the right of the individual to privacy. A typical example is the UK's Data Protection Act 1998: this governs the manner in which data relating to an individual can be stored, processed and disseminated, and establishes the rights of the data subject.

The Data Protection Act is founded on eight basic principles, as follows:

1   Fair and lawful processing: This requires that personal data must be obtained in a fair and open manner, that the subject of the data should be aware of the purpose of the data processing and that the processing itself must be fair and lawful.
2   Processing for a specified and lawful purpose: This requires that data may only be obtained and processed for one or more specified or lawful purposes, as defined in the Act.
3   Data not to be excessive: This requires that data should only be obtained and retained which is necessary to the nature of the processing.
4   Accuracy of data: This requires that data must be accurate and kept up to date.
5   Data not to be kept longer than necessary: This requires that data should only be retained for the period necessary to perform the processing.
6   Data subject rights: Data subjects have the right to be informed whether, and what, data is being processed, for what purpose, the recipients to whom the data may be disclosed and, in some cases, the source of the data.
7   Security: Data must be protected against unauthorized or unlawful processing, and from loss or damage. The level of security should be appropriate to the nature of the data and the potential harm that could arise from misuse.
8   Transfer outside the European Economic Area: Data may not be exported outside the European Economic Area except to a country that makes adequate provision for data protection.

Privacy legislation can have significant implications for any organization, in terms of both its operations and its collections. Archives in particular will almost inevitably hold quantities of information about private individuals. However, it should be noted that such legislation may well provide exemptions covering the processing of personal data for historical research purposes. This is certainly the case in the UK, where the Data Protection Act allows personal data to be preserved permanently for historical research purposes, if the data processing is not being used to support decisions about the data subject and is unlikely to cause substantial distress or damage. Furthermore, legitimate business interests which do not prejudice the rights, freedoms or interests of the data subject, together with statutory obligations, are considered legitimate purposes for data processing. It should also be noted that privacy legislation only applies to living persons.

Web archiving is less likely to be significantly affected by privacy legislation than other forms of collecting, for the simple reason that websites are normally already in the public domain, and therefore unlikely to hold material subject to such legislation. This is more likely to be an issue with intranets and the deep web. However, collecting organizations must be aware that they may be liable if they do archive websites that infringe privacy legislation.

Content liability and human rights

In addition to issues relating to the legality of obtaining, storing and disseminating web resources, organizations must also consider the legality of the content being collected. They must therefore take account of any liability to themselves that may arise from the archiving of web content. The most common forms of content liability relate to defamation, obscenity and the promotion of illegal activities. Liability may also arise from the act of making material available which could infringe a user's human rights.

Defamation

Defamation is the act of making false statements which cause damage to the reputation of a person. In many legal jurisdictions, a distinction is made between defamation through the spoken word, which is slander, and defamation via written communications, which is libel. However, the underlying distinction is based on the transience of the defamatory statement, and many jurisdictions therefore consider verbal comments which are broadcast, for example on radio or television, to be libel rather than slander.

In most jurisdictions, website owners are liable for defamatory material which they publish on their website, including material received from third parties. Furthermore, every viewing of that material counts as a new publication of the defamatory statement.

Obscenity

Legal definitions of obscenity may encompass a wide range of materials, including not only pornography but also violent and other potentially offensive content. Judgements as to what constitutes obscene material tend to be subjective, and generally require testing individually in a court of law. In the UK, the Obscene Publications Act 1959 states (s.1 (1)):

> An article shall be deemed to be obscene if its effect . . . is, if taken as a whole, such as to tend to deprave or corrupt persons who are likely . . . to read, see or hear the matter contained or embodied in it.

Also relevant in the UK is the Protection of Children Act 1978, amended by the Criminal Justice Act 1988, which makes it an offence to possess or distribute indecent photographs (including digital images) of children. The definition of 'indecent' is similarly left to the judgement of the courts.

Promotion of illegal activity

Website content may promote various forms of illegal activity. These might include the incitement of racial or religious hatred, or the promotion of terrorism. Although such content may contravene the laws of the country in which that material is hosted or accessible, a collecting institution may still wish to collect it as evidence of particular cultural attitudes and behaviours. An institution in this situation will need to consider very carefully whether either the collection or dissemination of such material would itself be illegal under its own governing laws. Even if collection is acceptable, it is almost certain that the options for delivery will be severely constrained, and that stringent safeguards will be required to limit access to legitimate users.

Human rights

Whether or not the content being collected is, of itself, illegal, care must be taken to ensure that its dissemination does not infringe human rights. For example, certain material could cause damage or distress to a user, and its availability will need to be controlled to provide adequate warning of its nature before it can be viewed, and to prevent accidental discovery. Access to some content may need to be restricted on the basis of criteria such as age and research credentials. It may even be the case that certain materials are inappropriate for delivery over the web at all, and must be limited to controlled on-site access within the collecting institution.

Defending against liability

Web archives may deliberately or accidentally collect and disseminate material that contravenes criminal or civil law, potentially within any jurisdiction. The most common scenario is likely to be that such material is inadvertently collected, with no deliberate intent on the part of the archive. However, such material does form part of the web's historical record, and may be of value to future researchers. Its very legality may even be judged differently in future. For these reasons, there may be cases where web archives wish to collect such material deliberately.

The legal situation in either case is far from clear-cut, and will differ considerably between jurisdictions. Nevertheless, a number of steps can be taken which may provide some degree of mitigation:

1   Preventing accidental collection: An archive may minimize the possibility of accidentally collecting illegal material through its selection policy and collection methods. For example, it might only collect from predetermined, selected websites, or configure its remote web crawler to avoid certain types of content. However, although evidence that the archive has taken active measures to prevent illegal material from being collected may offer some defence, such measures are not completely reliable.

2   Quality assurance: It may be possible to detect illegal material during the process of quality assurance. If an archive has reason to believe that

there is a significant risk, the assurance process can be designed accordingly.

3   Limiting access: The archive may instigate measures to limit access to those parts of the archive which might, for example, cause offence or distress. This may be difficult for material which is accessible online, as it may be difficult to verify the identity of the user with sufficient confidence. For example, online methods for restricting access based on age are virtually unenforceable, and therefore meaningless. Although search engines, web browsers and internet security software tools do increasingly offer content-based filtering, which allows access to certain types of material to be restricted, these are only enforceable client-side, and are therefore likely to offer little legal protection to the archive. A more robust alternative would be to restrict certain material to on-site access, where stricter controls and identification can be implemented.

4   'Take-down' policy: The archive should have in place a procedure to remove material which is reported to them as being in breach of the law. Action will need to be taken rapidly since, once notified, any defence of ignorance becomes invalid. In some cases, such as copyright, the archive will need to ensure that notification comes from a proper authority.

However, it must be stressed that any archive must take individual legal advice on these matters.

Enabling legislation
Archival legislation

Archival institutions, and especially national archives, are typically governed by some form of archival legislation, which defines statutory responsibilities for selecting, preserving, and providing access to archival records. Although the provisions of archival legislation vary considerably from country to country, the UK provides a typical example.

The National Archives of the UK are governed by the provisions of the Public Records Act 1958 (amended 1967). The Act makes provision for the proper management of public records, which are defined as the records of the government of the UK. This includes arrangements for the selection of records which are deemed to have historical value, for their preservation and for the provision of access to the public. The specific provisions of the Act with regard to copyright and public records are described in the previous section on intellectual property rights.

Legal deposit

In the library domain, legal deposit legislation fulfils a similar statutory role. It defines a legal obligation for publishers to deposit copies of all published works with designated libraries, in order to maintain a comprehensive collection of a nation's published output. The principle of legal deposit has a long history, dating back to 1537, when King François I of France issued the 'Ordonnance de Montpellier', which required a copy of every book to be deposited in the royal library before it could be sold.

The UK again provides a typical example. Legal deposit is governed by the Legal Deposit Libraries Act 2003, which requires publishers and distributors in the United Kingdom to send one copy of each of their publications to the Legal Deposit Office of the British Library within one month of publication. The Act covers all works published in the UK, as well as works originally published elsewhere but distributed in the UK, with the exception of certain defined categories, such as local transport timetables and examination papers. The Act, which replaces the previous Copyright Act 1911, includes electronic works within its definition of a publication. These may include offline electronic publications, such as CD-ROMs, and online publications, such as e-journals and websites. However, the procedures governing the deposit of electronic publications will need to be defined in a series of regulations to be brought forward under the Act. These regulations will be defined by an independent Legal Deposit Advisory Panel. Until such time as these regulations come into effect, the British Library is operating an interim arrangement, under the Voluntary Code of Practice 2000. Using this Code of Practice, the British Library is working closely with the UK publishing community to establish and encourage arrangements for the voluntary deposit of both offline and online electronic publications, and has already (as of 2005) received over 100,000 items.

Regulations governing the legal deposit of websites are not expected to come into effect for some time, and the UK national libraries have therefore focused on developing interim voluntary arrangements, principally under the auspices of the UK Web Archiving Consortium (see Chapter 2, The Development of Web Archiving). They have developed a standard procedure for seeking agreement from the identified owners of websites of interest for those websites to be collected, preserved, and made accessible by the national libraries. This includes a standard agreement, to be signed by the website owner, which is reproduced in Appendix 2. It should be noted that considerable efforts are devoted to securing these agreements, a process which can be complex and time-consuming, in order to ensure that all material is collected and made accessible with the explicit permission of the website's owner.

Regulatory compliance and public accountability
Compliance

Public and private organizations may be required to comply with a wide range of regulatory measures intended to provide transparency and accountability. Such measures may determine how long certain types of information must be retained, and whether information must be publicly disclosed. Examples of such regulations include the international Basel II Accord, and the Sarbanes-Oxley Act 2002 and the Health Insurance Portability and Accountability Act 1996 in the United States.

Although such measures may have a significant impact on the information an organization publishes on its website, and the length of time for which that information remains available, they are unlikely to affect web archiving programmes directly. However, they may provide a strong incentive for organizations to ensure proper management and archiving of their web content.

Freedom of information

Freedom of information legislation is concerned with the rights of individuals to access information created by the state. Such legislation has a long history: the first modern example comes from Sweden, where the

Principle of Public Access has been a fundamental part of the Swedish Constitution since 1766.

In the UK, the Freedom of Information Act 2000 came into full force on 1 January 2005, together with similar legislation covering Scotland. The Act defines rights of access to information held by public authorities, a definition which covers more than 100,000 organizations, and includes central and local government, the National Health Service, the police and local authority schools.

Its implications for library collections are minor since, by definition, published works are not subject to requests under freedom of information. On the other hand, it has profound implications for archives, and for the public bodies that create and transfer records to them. The Act replaces the access provisions previously defined in the Public Records Act 1958 (see above), and mandates access from the point of creation of a record, unless subject to a valid exemption.

The Act allows 24 exemptions, including:

- information accessible by other means
- information intended for future publication
- defence and national security
- national and international relations
- court records
- personal information
- commercial interests.

The practical application of the Act is governed by two Codes of Practice issued by the Lord Chancellor.[5] One sets out best practice for the handling of requests for information, and the other establishes best practice for bodies that create and actively manage information governed by the Act, and for archival institutions which hold records governed by the Act.

It should be noted that the Act requires the provision of information which answers the request made, rather than of an actual record. In general, public authorities have 20 working days to respond to requests, and requesters can appeal to the Information Commissioner if they feel that a request has been wrongly rejected.

In the UK, rights of access to environmental information are subject to the separate provisions of the Environmental Information Regulations 2004, which implement EU Directive 2003/4/EC. These regulations, and equivalent implementations of the EU Directive in the national legislative frameworks of other EU member states, are broadly similar in principles and practice to the Freedom of Information Act.

However, freedom of information legislation should have relatively minor implications for web archiving, as most websites are already available in the public domain. The exceptions to this will be intranets, and websites to which access is controlled. Here, the main consideration will be that, if the archive is subject to freedom of information, there may be a potential conflict if it wishes to collect material from a non-freedom of information body, as the archive may be required to disclose any information held in its collections.

Conclusion

The legal implications of undertaking web archiving are potentially very complex, and should not be overlooked. This chapter is intended to provide no more than a rapid overview of the main areas of law which are likely to be applicable. For more detailed advice, the reader is encouraged to consult more specialist sources of advice, such as those mentioned in the text. Excellent assessments of the legal implications of web archiving have been published recently.[6] However, for any organization considering the archiving of web content, the most important recommendation must be:

If in doubt, seek legal advice.

Notes and references

1   See www.fsf.org/licenses/fdl.html [accessed 19 February 2006].

2   See http://creativecommons.org/ [accessed 19 February 2006].

3   Christensen-Dalsgaard, B., Fønss-Jørgensen, E., von Hielmcrone, H., Finneman, N. O., Brügger, N., Henriksen, B. and Carlsen, S. V. (2003) *Experiences and Conclusions from a Pilot Study: web archiving of the district and county elections 2001 - final report for the pilot project 'netarkivet.dk' (English version)*, Statsbiblioteket and Kongelige Bibliotek, Denmark,

http://netarkivet.dk/rap/webark-final-rapport-2003.pdf [accessed 18 February 2006].

4   Padfield, T. (2004) *Copyright for Archivists and Users of Archives*, 2nd edn, Facet Publishing.

5   Great Britain, Department for Constitutional Affairs (2002) *Lord Chancellor's Code of Practice on the Management of Records. Issued under section 46 of the Freedom of Information Act 2000.*
     Great Britain, Department for Constitutional Affairs (2004) *Secretary of State for Constitutional Affairs' Code of Practice on the Discharge of Public Authorities' Functions under Part I of the Freedom of Information Act 2000. Issued under section 45 of the Act.*

6   Borrull, A. L. and Oppenheim, C. (2004) Legal aspects of the Web, *Annual Review of Information Science and Technology*, **38**, 483-548; Charlesworth, A. (2003) *Legal Issues Relating to the Archiving of Internet Resources in the UK, EU, USA and Australia: a study undertaken for the JISC and the Wellcome Trust*, University of Bristol, www.jisc.ac.uk/uploaded_documents/archiving_legal.pdf [accessed 19 February 2006].

Chapter 9

Managing a web archiving programme

Introduction

This chapter describes the practicalities of establishing, resourcing and maintaining a web archiving programme. It discusses the variety of operational models available, the relative merits and disadvantages of each, and the factors that might influence the selection of the most appropriate strategy. It examines management issues and identifies the range of staff skills required. It concludes with a case study provided by the web archiving programme developed by The National Archives of the UK (TNA), which offers a practical example of how one such a programme was established and developed in recent years.

Alternative operational models

A number of different models have emerged for developing and implementing a web archiving programme. These can be broadly categorized as follows:

- in-house: programmes are entirely resourced, managed and implemented within the organization
- contracted-out: programmes have all or some aspects of the work performed by a contractor

- consortia: programmes are implemented by a consortium of organiz-ations, using some degree of shared infrastructure.

Each of these models is discussed in detail below. Every approach has specific advantages and disadvantages and, in practice, many organizations choose to implement programmes that include elements from more than one model.

The in-house model

A web archiving programme which is implemented and operated entirely using in-house resources does, in principle, offer the greatest flexibility and control. However, it also places the entire burden of risk on the organization, and the complexities involved mean that this is not an option to be undertaken lightly.

Clearly, this option is only viable if the necessary skills, infrastructure and other resources for each stage of the programme are either already available in-house, or can be realistically developed. As such, in-house programmes tend to be the province either of very large organizations, or of those with very small-scale programmes.

The contracted-out model

An organization may not wish to invest in establishing all of the infrastructure and other resources required to undertake web archiving in-house. In this case, contracting out some or all elements of the programme may be an attractive option. It may be possible to use a contractor with existing experience in the field, but there is a limited pool available and it is equally possible to use a contractor with transferable skills. For example, TNA has used the services of the Internet Archive, arguably the most experienced operator in the field, but the UK Web Archiving Consortium chose a contractor with no direct web archiving experience but which did have substantial experience in web hosting, large-scale data storage and web crawling for search purposes.

The suitability of this approach may also be influenced by the scale of the planned programme. Larger programmes are likely to be more attractive to contractors, and offer greater opportunities for customizing the service to the individual needs of the organization. A very small programme may simply not be viable as a contracted-out service. On the other hand, the process of setting up a large contract can be time-consuming and burdensome and, for public sector organizations, is strictly regulated.

Contracting does transfer some of the risk to the contractor, and the expertise of a skilled contractor can be a very valuable asset. On the other hand, the management of a major contract will require dedicated staff resources. The success of this approach is very dependent upon choosing the right contractor, and the importance of establishing an appropriate contract, together with the time and expertise required to draft, negotiate and implement it, should not be underestimated.

The consortium model

In the consortium model, a number of different organizations, with a common requirement for a web archiving capability, join forces to create a shared service. Typically, this involves sharing the development costs and operational use of some, or all, of the necessary infrastructure.

The advantages of this approach include:

1   Shared risk: The programme risk is shared among the partners, rather than borne entirely by one institution.
2   Shared expertise: Each partner can benefit from the expertise of other partners. This will be particularly apparent if each partner brings different and complementary expertise to the consortium.
3   Co-ordinated collecting: By collaborating, the partners can ensure that individual collection policies are co-ordinated and complementary. This can minimize the risk of unnecessary duplication of effort or, equally, of accidental gaps in collection coverage.
4   Virtual collections: Partners can also collaborate on developing virtual collections of related material, with each partner contributing content within their area of interest. Such virtual collections can offer greater value as a whole than would be achievable within the more confined collecting remit of a single organization.

As with any approach, there are also potential disadvantages to be considered:

1   Complexity: By definition, a collaborative approach brings an additional level of complexity. Significant decisions will need to be agreed by all partners, which may reduce the speed and responsiveness of operations. Greater resources are also likely to be required to provide co-ordination at both strategic and operational levels.
2   Shared control: Collaboration also requires that partners surrender some degree of control. This can create additional risks and dependencies which are beyond the means of any one partner to mitigate. For example, the unexpected withdrawal of a critical partner from the consortium might threaten the entire programme.

A consortium may be established on a temporary or a permanent basis, and will require some form of consortium agreement. The complexity of such an agreement will depend upon the nature of the planned consortium: for example, a consortium which is planned as a permanent or long-term body with independent legal status will require some form of legal contract, whereas for a less formal or temporary body, some form of Memorandum of Understanding may suffice. Whatever the nature of the agreement, it will certainly need to cover the following:

1   Purpose and duration: A clear description of the overall purpose of the consortium, and of the planned duration of the agreement, must be agreed.
2   Management structure: A description is needed of the management structure for the consortium. This will need to include some form of management committee, with rules for appointing a chair and secretary. It should define rules for the operation of that structure, such as quoracy, partner representation and voting rights. It may also be necessary to define separate arrangements for project management and working groups.

3 Membership: The membership of the consortium must be defined, together with arrangements for accepting new members and for the departure of existing partners.

4 Responsibilities of partners: A definition of the fundamental responsibilities and obligations of partners must be agreed.

5 Costs: Any financial arrangements must be defined, including all financial contributions required from partners, and a payment profile for these contributions.

6 Intellectual property: Arrangements for the management of intellectual property must be defined, including intellectual property that partners contribute to the consortium, intellectual property that arises from the work of the consortium, and third-party intellectual property that may be used by the consortium.

7 Liabilities: The extent of any liabilities that each party will bear must be defined.

8 Confidentiality: The agreement must clearly define any confidentiality agreements to which the parties will be subject.

9 Termination: A definition will be required of the circumstances in which the agreement may be terminated, either for a single party or for all parties.

10 Consortium description: A description of the proposed scope and nature of the work of the consortium, with relevant deliverables and timetables, must also be agreed upon.

An agreement which takes the form of a legal contract will additionally need to cover issues such a governing law, *force majeure*, dispute resolution and the assignment of contract rights and obligations. The length of time required to develop and agree such a document should not be underestimated, especially if the member institutions are very diverse.

Once the consortium has been established, the shared infrastructure must be developed. Any of the other models may be adopted for this: the infrastructure could be hosted by one partner, contracted out on behalf of the consortium or distributed among all the partners. The factors influencing this decision will be the same as those faced by a single organization. The consortium model can be illustrated by the case study of the UK Web Archiving Consortium.

Case study: the UK Web Archiving Consortium

An example of the consortium approach is provided by the UK Web Archiving Consortium. In 2003, a number of institutions within the UK began to discuss their common requirements for web archiving. Although several of them, including TNA and the British Library, were already engaged in their own programmes, there was general recognition that a collaborative approach could be beneficial. This was confirmed by a report jointly commissioned by the Joint Information Systems Committee of the UK further and higher education funding councils (JISC) and the Wellcome Trust.[1] This recommended that JISC and Wellcome should seek to work with other partners to create a pilot web archiving service, not only to realize economies of scale, but also to demonstrate the benefits of such collaboration.

As a result, the UK Web Archiving Consortium was established in late 2003. It currently comprises six members: the British Library, The National Archives, the National Libraries of Wales and Scotland, JISC and the Wellcome Trust. The initial goal of the consortium was to conduct a two-year pilot project to develop and evaluate a collaborative infrastructure for selective web archiving. This project was formally launched in June 2004. After consideration of the various options, the PANDAS system, developed by the National Library of Australia, and described in detail in Chapter 4, Collection Methods, was chosen for the pilot. The task of modifying PANDAS for consortium use, and for hosting the software and the collected data, was contracted out to a third-party supplier.

Initial development work focused on modifications to PANDAS, including enhancements to the public interface and the provision of search facilities. In parallel with this, the consortium began to develop an integrated collecting policy based on the individual policies of all partners, in order to co-ordinate the exact scope of each partner's future collecting. With the exception of The National Archives, all partners were required to obtain explicit agreement from website owners before each site could be harvested. The development of an appropriate process for securing such permissions, supported by a standard copyright licence agreement, was therefore a priority (see Appendix 2).

Once PANDAS was available for use by the consortium, and the permissions process was in operation, partners began extensive testing of the system, including collecting, processing and cataloguing a wide range of websites. The UKWAC web archive was publicly launched in May 2005 (see Figure 9.1), marking the point at which the system was considered ready for operational use, and a significant volume of websites had been collected. Since that time, the consortium has continued to collect and make available a wide range of websites from the UK domain and, by early 2006, had archived over 1000 unique websites.

A notable feature of the consortium has been the development of thematic collections, to which individual partners contribute sites within their sphere of interest, to create a virtual collection which surpasses any one partner's collecting remit. One such example is the 2004 Tsunami collection: The National Archives collected key government websites, the Wellcome Trust collected relevant public health sites and the various national libraries collected a diverse range of sites reflecting political,

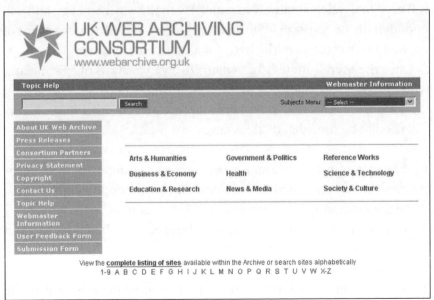

Figure 9.1   The UKWAC web archive (UK Web Archiving Consortium)

religious and economic responses to the disaster.[2] Other thematic collections have covered the 2005 general election, and the 2005 G8 summit at Gleneagles.

The pilot project is due to conclude in June 2006 and, prior to that, UKWAC is preparing an evaluation report, including recommendations for the future. Although the findings of that report cannot be prejudged, the consortium has undoubtedly provided a valuable insight into the benefits of collaborative working. It is unarguable that the consortium has enabled a number of organizations to engage in web archiving on a scale that would not otherwise have been possible.

Selecting and implementing a model

Any decision about the actual model, or models, to be adopted must proceed from an analysis of an organization's requirements. Having identified the need for some form of web archiving programme, the very first step for any organization should therefore be to begin developing an overall strategy. This should define the aims and ambitions of the programme and its envisaged scope, scale and duration. The definition of a collecting policy for websites should be an early goal: although this will need to develop iteratively in parallel with the wider strategy, and will undoubtedly be constrained to some degree by a realistic assessment of the options, it must form the basis for all future decisions.

Once the overall strategy has emerged, a gap analysis of existing and required resources, informed by strategic business need, should be used to inform an evaluation of the possible approaches. A number of key factors will need to be considered, including:

1   Existing infrastructure and expertise: The availability of existing, or easily procured, expertise and infrastructure to support each element of the programme must be assessed. This may include the availability of suitable third-party suppliers and contractors. It is possible, and indeed likely, that different models may be suitable for each element. This is considered in more detail later in this section.

2   Desired speed of implementation: The urgency with which the programme must be implemented should be assessed. This will need

to be weighed against the likely costs associated with different timescales. Depending on the point from which an organization is starting, different models are likely to be achievable over varying timescales. For example, it may be expedient to use a contractor at the outset, even if the longer-term strategic aim is to develop in-house facilities.

3   Costs: The cost-effectiveness of different models should be considered, over both the short and the long term. For smaller-scale web archiving programmes, it may be more cost-effective to use a contractor than to develop in-house facilities, although in-house or consortium approaches may prove to be more economical in the long term.

4   Legal and strategic priorities: There may be legal requirements or organizational priorities that place restrictions on the choice of model. For example, there may be limitations on which elements can be contracted out; material to which access restrictions apply may need to be managed in-house.

5   Acceptable risk: Organizations will vary in terms of the level and nature of risk they will consider acceptable for any activity, and a thorough risk assessment should be performed for each model under consideration.

These factors may influence the overall approach. However, each element of the proposed programme will also need detailed individual consideration. An analysis of some of respective merits and disadvantages of the three models follows.

Selection

It is almost inevitable that an organization will wish to retain full control of the selection process, although it may be conceivable, in some circumstances, for a contractor to undertake detailed selection tasks in accordance with defined selection policies. Either the in-house or consortium models are therefore suitable options, with the latter offering particular advantages as a number of other organizations may have overlapping collecting interests.

Collection

Collection is a prime candidate for a contracted-out service, being a technically specialized and potentially resource-intensive process. The availability of existing tools for this also increases its viability as an outsourced service. The consortium approach is also a strong option and, although it does require in-house access to technical expertise, there is greater opportunity for sharing such expertise between partners. Collection is only a suitable in-house option if appropriate technical expertise and infrastructure can be deployed.

Quality assurance

An organization will always need to undertake a degree of quality assurance for itself. However, it would be desirable for any contractor to undertake rigorous QA tasks as part of their service. For example, a contractor providing collection services could reasonably be expected to quality assure the material collected, before passing it to the customer for acceptance. An in-house approach will always therefore be required, although elements of this function can potentially be undertaken using the contracted-out or consortium models as well.

Preservation

Passive preservation (i.e. data storage) and active preservation may both be impractical as in-house activities, although for different reasons. Data volumes are likely to be the main determining factor for passive preservation, whereas for active preservation the very specialized technical demands will be more significant. It is likely that full-scale digital preservation services will only be a viable in-house option for the largest organizations, and for those which have preservation as a core strategic goal. Contracting out is most likely to be a realistic choice for passive preservation, since at the present time commercial providers of active preservation services are virtually non-existent. However, it is likely, over time, that organizations will increasingly be able to utilize specific third-party preservation services, many of which may be available on a non-commercial basis (e.g. TNA's PRONOM service, described in Chapter 6, Preservation). Issues of curatorial responsibility may also influence decisions in this area. Consortium approaches, which combine individual organizational control with collaborative development of specialized services, may prove the most effective option in many cases.

Delivery

Delivery is likely to be suited to the in-house approach if an organization already has an established web-hosting infrastructure. However, an existing website infrastructure does not, in itself, provide such capability. Even a relatively modest web archiving programme can quickly generate terabyte-scale collections, requiring expensive and specialized online storage systems. Equally, usage demands may require bandwidth and availability levels which are impractical for the organization to meet. Other models are therefore more appropriate where the data volumes and usage levels exceed an organization's capabilities, or for organizations with no existing in-house capabilities.

The applicability of each model to the major web archiving functions is summarized in Table 9.1.

Table 9.1   Comparison of management models

	In-house	Contracted-out	Consortium
Selection	Yes	No	Yes
Collection	Yes – if infrastructure and resources available	Yes	Yes
QA	Yes	Yes – in conjunction with in-house QA	Yes – in conjunction with in-house QA
Preservation	Yes – if existing expertise available	Yes – primarily for passive preservation	Yes
Delivery	Yes – if infrastructure and resources available	Yes	Yes

Implementing the programme

An analysis of the available options should allow the selection of an appropriate model for each function. In the case of contracted-out approaches, this analysis will also enable the development of a clear statement of requirements, which will form the basis for selecting an appropriate contractor and monitoring their subsequent performance.

Unless the programme is intended to be of permanent duration, an exit strategy should also be developed. Even if the overall programme does not have a defined end, any individual elements which are dependent on third parties will still require such a strategy. This is particularly important when using a contractor, as this is, by definition, a solution with a fixed duration. It is therefore essential to define an exit strategy at the outset, which covers both planned and unplanned termination of the contract.

The exit strategy should influence the choice of standards to be followed, and in particular those relating to the manner in which the collection is stored. This is essential to avoid any dependence upon a particular solution, such as that provided by a contractor, beyond the planned term, and to simplify any future transition to a different contractor or to an alternative service model. For example, it is strongly recommended that the use of proprietary metadata schemes or storage formats be avoided.

Managing the programme

In order for an operational programme to be implemented, the organization will need to identify business owners for each of the key functions, as follows:

1   Selection: This will include liaison with website owners and the securing of any necessary permission agreements.
2   Collection: Depending on the approach adopted, this may comprise operational or contract management.
3   Quality assurance: This could be combined with collection, but it is desirable for QA to be undertaken separately if possible.
4   Preservation: This may use a combination of in-house and externally-provided services.

5   Delivery: This includes both the technical aspects of delivery and more general engagement with the user community.

Depending on the size of the organization, and the scale of the programme, some or all of these functions may be combined under a single business owner, and may have very different numbers of staff allocated to them. However, for even the smallest programme, it is strongly recommended that at least one full-time staff post be given dedicated responsibility for web archiving. In practice, the use of at least a proportion of a number of other posts is likely to be required. As an example, TNA employs approximately 550 full-time staff in total. One full-time post is dedicated to the web archiving programme, with four other posts providing 25% each. Allowing for additional staff time for general infrastructure support, such as IT staff and webmasters, suggests a total staff requirement of three full-time equivalents. In addition to this, a substantial proportion of an estimated five posts is provided by various external contractors.

The technical infrastructure and staff skills required for operational management are discussed in the following sections.

Technical infrastructure

The requirements for technical infrastructure to support web archiving are concentrated in three areas: collection, preservation and delivery.

Collection

The requirements here will vary according to the collection methods used. For contracted-out services there should be no infrastructure requirements beyond the likely need for an internet connection to allow remote quality assurance of new material.

Requirements under the consortium model will vary depending on the exact approach adopted. However, it is likely that access to the shared infrastructure will be provided as an online service. As such, the main requirement will again be for internet connectivity, although the potentially more burdensome demands of using such a service may require greater available bandwidth for the connection.

The greatest infrastructure demands are clearly imposed by in-house web archiving. These will vary depending on the collection method adopted. Remote harvesting, database archiving and transactional archiving will all require a high-bandwidth internet connection, and dedicated servers for data storage and hosting collection tools such as web crawlers. Direct transfer methods are typically less demanding, but will still require server space and appropriate operating system and application infrastructure, to allow the collected sites to be reconstructed and stored.

In all models, additional infrastructure will be required to support any workflow management application that may be used to monitor the overall collection process.

The majority of the infrastructure required for web archiving will use standard, commodity hardware and software, and should present few inherent challenges for any organization with a well-developed IT infrastructure. However, installation and maintenance of some of the more specialized web archiving software tools may require skills less common within typical IT departments. Many of these tools are developed by open-source communities, and run in operating system environments such as Linux. As such, they may be atypical of the applications that IT departments normally support, and therefore require the development of new skills.

Preservation

Digital preservation requires significant specialized technical infrastructure, which is discussed in detail in Chapter 6. However, website preservation does not require any additional facilities. Therefore, if an organization has a broader remit for preserving digital content, and has already made provision for preservation facilities, these can certainly be utilized for web archiving.

A degree of passive preservation capability can be achieved through the adaptation of existing data storage systems, but active preservation will require the development of specialized new systems, and may only be feasible for larger organizations.

Delivery

The infrastructure requirements for delivery are essentially the same as for any website; in other words, an organization which already hosts its own website should, in principle, not require a substantially different infrastructure. In practice, there are likely to be two possible additional considerations. First, there is the question of scale: although primarily a storage issue (as discussed in the previous section), the online delivery of very large volumes of data will undoubtedly have an impact in terms of web server capacity and connection bandwidth. Second, specialized software may be used to provide access to the collection (see Chapter 7, Delivery to Users), which will require staff skills for installation and support.

For organizations that rely on a third-party internet service provider (ISP) to host their website, the same issues will apply, but the extent to which the ISP may be willing or able to meet the additional demands will need to be investigated. It is certainly likely that a substantial increase in data storage or user traffic requirements will have resource implications for any third-party hosting contract.

Staff skills

As this is a relatively new discipline, the available pool of potential staff with direct web archiving expertise is likely to be relatively small. However, there is considerable crossover with skills available in other disciplines, although a degree of creativity and flexibility may be required to identify where this is likely to occur. Web-specific technical skills, which will be essential to support the technical aspects of collection, preservation and delivery, are, of course, widely available within the IT sector. Equally, existing selection and curatorial skills should transfer directly. Digital preservation skills are, as yet, a scarce commodity, but a combination of enthusiasm and widespread knowledge sharing between those already engaged in this field can help to overcome this.

It may prove difficult to recruit individuals who combine the breadth of necessary skills and, in this respect, a larger team of specialists may be easier to establish than a smaller team of generalists. Organizations should also review their existing skills base, as many of the required areas of expertise may already be available in-house.

The types of post required to support a web archiving programme will vary considerably, depending on the scale of the programme and the operational model adopted. An example job description for a 'general purpose' web archivist is given in Appendix 5. In some instances, aspects of this role might be split between a number of more specialized posts.

The UK Government Web Archive: a case study

The National Archives of the UK (TNA) established its web archiving programme in 2003, in response to two targets set by the UK government as part of its e-government agenda. The 1999 *Modernizing Government* White Paper set targets that all newly-created public records be electronically stored and retrieved by 2004, and that all government services to the citizen and to business should be available online by 2008. The latter target was subsequently advanced to 2005.

Although it had previously been recognized that individual documents contained in government websites could be public records, the pervasiveness of electronic service delivery across the UK government led TNA to conclude that the websites themselves should be considered public records. The distinction here is significant: the requirement was not simply to collect and preserve individual documents, but to capture the changing nature of the interaction between the state and its citizens in an online environment. This could only be achieved through a broadly-based programme to archive government websites.

TNA's initial, experimental step into the world of web archiving came in 2001, when a decision was made to capture a snapshot of the Prime Minister's website on 6 June 2001, the day before the general election. The site was collected by direct transfer, and the process is described in detail in Chapter 4, Collection Methods. This experience confirmed both that TNA should engage in a broadly-based web archiving programme and that, to be practical, such a programme would need to be developed in a systematic manner.

Before a practical programme could be implemented, it was necessary to establish the scope of the desired collection. TNA therefore drafted an operational selection policy for government websites[3] which, after public consultation, was formally adopted. The method of selection adopted was appraisal by categorization. A high-level analysis of the overall functions of government identified six main categories, as follows:

- defence and foreign policy
- the administration of justice and internal security
- the management of national resources
- the provision of services not provided by the market (e.g. health, education and culture)
- the regulation and co-ordination of market-provided services
- the machinery of government and delegated administrations.

A representative sample of websites was then identified within each category. This included all major central government departments (i.e. those headed by Cabinet Ministers), together with a selection of executive agencies and other government bodies.

It was recognized that the rate at which the content of these websites changes can vary considerably, and that a flexible approach to the frequency of collection was therefore required. At the same time, the collection programme would need to be manageable. Two basic collection frequencies were therefore adopted: the majority of websites would be collected on a six-monthly basis, but the most dynamic and significant sites would be sampled weekly. However, for specific cases, other sampling frequencies, such as quarterly collection, are also used. The sampling frequency can also be changed in response to current events. For example, as concerns grew about the possible spread of avian flu in late 2005, the frequency of collecting public health websites was temporarily increased.

The operational selection policy (OSP) therefore provides the criteria that enable a detailed collection list to be defined and maintained. This list documents the current set of websites to be collected, including the URLs that define the collecting boundaries, and the sampling frequency for each website.

The OSP provides the framework for selecting websites across the whole central government domain, providing regular snapshots of the development of e-government as a whole. However, individual websites may also be selected for very specific reasons, governed by other OSPs. For example, public inquiries – government-instigated formal investigations into events such as major disasters – now use the web as a major channel for reporting to the public. An Inquiry will typically establish a website which will contain not only the final report of its findings, but also the detailed evidence presented to it and transcripts of the actual hearings. Collection of inquiry websites is therefore becoming the standard means by which TNA acquires these records. Being of fixed duration, an inquiry website will normally be collected once, after the final report has been published. However, for high-profile inquiries, the site may also be sampled at intervals while the hearings are in progress. These additional websites are incorporated into the collection list.

Having established the scope of its web archiving programme, TNA then began to investigate methods of implementation. The initial collection list developed in 2003 contained 55 websites, of which ten were to be collected on a weekly basis. Remote harvesting was chosen as the most appropriate collection strategy, as it was considered to offer the best balance between practicality and quality. In the context of a selection policy which sought to develop a broadly-based picture of the UK central government domain, it was considered more appropriate to adopt an approach capable of high-volume collection at an acceptable level of quality, rather than more labour-intensive methods, such as direct transfer, which might offer limited gains in quality but would not be sustainable for the quantity of material.

At the time, it was not considered feasible for TNA to undertake such a programme in-house: this would have required significant investment in staff skills and infrastructure, and the risks of doing so immediately were not justifiable. TNA therefore negotiated a contract with the Internet Archive (see Chapter 2, The Development of Web Archiving) to collect and deliver websites on TNA's behalf. TNA determined the sites to be collected and the frequency, based on the collection list, performed quality assurance and created a portal to the resultant collection on its website (see Figure 9.2).

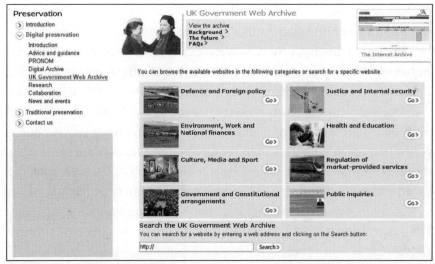

Figure 9.2 The UK Government Web Archive (The National Archives)

The Internet Archive performed the actual harvesting, stored the collected sites on its own servers and provided public access to the collection.

Adopting the contracted-out approach enabled TNA to establish a web archiving programme of significant scale in a very short timeframe. It also provided a forum for staff to gain skills and experience in the technical and organizational aspects of web archiving. The contract was designed to provide flexibility, allowing the actual crawl list to be changed as required. It also allowed the scope of the collection to be increased over time, and was based on a transparent charging structure. The contract was agreed on an annual basis: this was important given the developmental nature of the programme, and the fact that TNA was still evolving its longer-term strategy for web archiving.

The Internet Archive contract proved very successful, allowing the rapid collection and dissemination of a large collection of websites. However, TNA was also keen to develop an in-house web archiving capability. Although the service provided by the Internet Archive was very responsive, allowing rapid adaptation to changing events, the nature of a contracted-out service does place inherent limitations on that flexibility. In addition, with electronic records becoming a key strategic priority for

TNA, it was considered essential that such an important programme should not be entirely dependent upon an external service provider.

The establishment of the UK Web Archiving Consortium (described earlier in this chapter), of which TNA was a founding member, provided the opportunity to advance this ambition. UKWAC provided TNA with the necessary infrastructure to harvest websites under the direct control of its own staff. This second strand of the web archiving programme is very much complementary to the contracted-out service. The large-scale, repeated collection of the core website list is still most effectively achieved by an external supplier, but the in-house capability is harnessed for infrequent or 'one-off' collecting, and to provide a rapid-response capability. For example, most public inquiry websites are now collected through UKWAC.

In 2005, a new organization, the European Archive, was established with the support of the Internet Archive, which offered equivalent capabilities (see Chapter 2, The Development of Web Archiving). At the Internet Archives' suggestion, TNA transferred its contracted-out service to the European Archive at the end of 2005. For the Internet Archive, the establishment of mirror services in other parts of the world is important for securing a sustainable global web archive; for TNA, using a more locally-based contractor offers practical advantages in terms of contract management.

Operational responsibility for web archiving is divided between two TNA departments. The Records Management Department (RMD) is responsible for the appraisal, selection and transfer of records to TNA, owns the operational selection policy and maintains the collection list through a process of research and consultation. The Digital Preservation Department (DPD) manages the web archiving programme, and is responsible for collection, quality assurance, preservation and delivery. DPD ensures that the selected websites are collected to required standards, and remain available to users. Its responsibilities therefore include management of external contracts, representation on the management board of UKWAC and the provision of in-house technical staff.

By the end of 2005, two years after the programme was started, the UK Government Web Archive collection contained over 20 million web pages, amounting to over one terabyte of data. A quarter of a million new pages are added every week. The collection has also established a growing user base, and, given that the majority of the collection is very recent, and that it may be expected that greatest interest will attach to the older material, it is anticipated that user interest will increase considerably over time. TNA has also worked to engage with its suppliers – the webmasters who manage government websites. Not only has it established standards for good practice in creating 'archive-friendly' websites,[4] but it has also encouraged the active participation of websites, through mechanisms such as the 'Archived by The National Archives' logo (described in Chapter 7, Delivery to Users). TNA has adopted a pragmatic approach to web archiving, combining different models of service provision to establish a flexible programme that meets its strategic and operational goals, and which is also achievable within the available resources.

Notes and references

1   Day, M. (2003) *Collecting and Preserving the World Wide Web: a feasibility study undertaken for the JISC and Wellcome Trust*, JISC and Wellcome Trust, http://library.welcome.ac.uk/assets/wtl039229.pdf [accessed 23 October 2005].

2   The collection is available at www.webarchive.org.uk/col/c8050.html [accessed 19 February 2006].

3   The National Archives (2003) *Operational Selection Policy 27: the selection of government websites*, www.nationalarchives.gov.uk/recordsmanagement/selection/pdf/osp27.pdf [accessed 29 October 2005].

4   Office of the e-Envoy (2003) *Guidelines for UK Government Websites: illustrated handbook for web management teams*, The Stationery Office, www.cabinetoffice.gov.uk/e-government/resources/handbook/introduction.asp [accessed 19 February 2006].

Chapter 10
Future trends

Introduction

Attempting to forecast future trends, especially in such a rapidly changing and unpredictable field as information technology, is a notoriously inexact science. Nonetheless, there are at least some forecasts that may be usefully made in this area. This chapter examines some of the likely advances that will be made over the next few years, in the areas of data storage, digital preservation, web archiving, and the very shape of the world wide web itself.

Data storage

Web archiving can generate very large volumes of data, which need to be stored and managed. The largest web archives are already approaching or exceeding the petabyte level (1,000 terabytes). In the near future, the larger web archives will be measured in tens or hundreds of petabytes, which will test the limits of current storage technologies. Fortunately, storage capacities show every sign of continuing to rise, accompanied by commensurate reductions in costs, at their current rate for the foreseeable future. Equally, new and more efficient types of storage technology will undoubtedly emerge.

The storage capacities of established technologies, such as hard disk and magnetic tape, are continuing to increase significantly. In 2005, single hard disks with 500 gigabyte capacities were widely available. New technologies such as perpendicular recording, where data is recorded in three-dimensional columns rather than on the two-dimensional disk surface, are expected to increase capacities tenfold over the next few years.

Magnetic tape remains the most common choice for very large data volumes. To illustrate the progression of storage capacities, one of the most widely used tape formats is linear tape open (LTO). The first generation of LTO cartridge, released in 1999, could store 100 gigabytes of uncompressed data. By 2002, the second generation offered 200 gigabyte capacities. The current LTO 3 format boasts 400 gigabytes per tape, with 800 GB expected by 2009 and 3.2 TB beyond that.

Flash memory is also becoming increasingly widespread. Although traditionally confined to portable devices such as music players and removable 'memory sticks', the first Flash-based hard drives are now being developed. Although initially aimed at the laptop market, such devices may well become ubiquitous.

Another promising area of research is the application of micro-electromechanical systems (MEMS) to data storage. MEMS devices are mechanical components created using micrometre- and nanometre-scale manufacturing technologies. IBM recently demonstrated a prototype system called Millipede,[1] which uses atomic force probes to create nanometre-scale indentations in a polymer film. The indentations can be erased by melting areas of the film, creating a read–write storage medium. MEMS storage could offer huge capacities, well beyond the expected limits of magnetic storage. The prototype has achieved densities of more than one terabit per square inch, the equivalent of storing over 100 gigabytes on an area the size of a postage stamp.

One of the most exciting prospects is holographic storage, which is likely to become a mainstream technology within the next few years. Information is encoded as a 'checkerboard' pattern of binary data. This data is written to the storage medium using a laser, which is split into two separate beams. The signal beam carries the pattern of encoded data, while a second, reference beam intersects the signal beam, creating an interference pattern which forms a hologram. At the point of intersection between the two beams, the interference pattern is recorded on a photosensitive layer within the recording medium. By varying the angle or wavelength of the reference beam, many holograms can be stored at various depths within the recording medium; it is the ability to store data in three dimensions, throughout the depth of the recording layer, which yields the huge potential storage capacities of holographic media.

The data is read by using the same reference laser beam to detect the recorded interference pattern. Because the entire hologram can be written and read in parallel using a single flash of laser light, rather than one bit at a time, holographic storage also offers very fast data transfer rates. Several vendors are already developing commercial holographic storage products, the first generations of which are expected to appear by the end of 2006. These first media are likely to offer capacities of 200 gigabytes on a DVD-size disk, but later generations are expected to provide over one terabyte per disk. A number of different, competing technologies are being developed and, as with DVD and CD, it is likely to be some time before one single standard emerges. Nevertheless, over the next few years holographic media may well become a serious competitor to magnetic disk and tape in the data storage market.

Storage capacity is not the only challenge: multi-petabyte archives create significant storage management challenges. Innovations here are likely to be driven primarily by the scientific and commercial sectors. Although web archiving can generate large data volumes, it is dwarfed in this respect by scientific research activities such as particle physics, meteorology and bioscience. To give some examples:

1   The Large Hadron Collider is the latest particle accelerator to be built at CERN, the European Organization for Nuclear Research. When it becomes operational in 2007, it is expected to generate 15 petabytes of data each year, and the total data generated from experiments is expected to eventually exceed one exabyte (one million terabytes).[2]

2   The European Centre for Medium-Range Weather Forecasts currently holds over 1.5 PB of meteorological data.[3]

3   The European Space Agency maintains a historical archive of data from
    Earth observation satellites at its ESRIN site. This archive contains two
    petabytes of data, as of 2005, and is growing at a rate of 400 terabytes
    per year.[4]

In the world of e-science, the challenge will be to scale up to exabyte-level
data storage facilities within the next few years.[5] In the commercial world,
the requirement to retain e-mails for regulatory compliance is generating
massive e-mail archives. The pharmaceutical and petroleum exploration
industries also create huge data volumes that require management. For
example, a single seismic survey can produce one petabyte of data.

The response of both commercial storage developers and academic
research to these challenges should provide data storage solutions that
will also meet the requirements of web archiving programmes.

Digital preservation

The next few years will undoubtedly bring major advances in the theory
and practice of digital preservation and, in particular, in the development
of a wide range of new tools. Some of the preservation tools which are
already available or under development have been discussed in Chapter
6, Preservation. It is to be hoped and anticipated that future preservation
tool development will enjoy a similar convergence, in terms of standards
and interoperability, to that already being exhibited with web archiving
tools. The major foci for current and future development are likely to
include work within individual cultural memory institutions, international
collaboration and standards development.

Cultural memory institutions

Major archival institutions and libraries are committing significant
resources to the development of digital preservation facilities. The United
States provides two such examples. The National Digital Information
Infrastructure and Preservation Programme (NDIIPP) is being led by
the Library of Congress, with funding worth $99.8 million.[6] The Library
is working with a range of partners in the public and private sector to
develop a national strategy to collect and preserve important digital

resources for future generations. Also in 2005 the National Archives and Records Administration (NARA) announced the award of a contract worth $308 million to develop its Electronic Records Archives.[7] This programme, which will run until 2012, will provide NARA with the capability to preserve electronic records. It may be expected that both programmes will produce wider benefits and advances in the field of digital preservation.

Other notable examples of the development of operational digital preservation systems include The National Archives' Seamless Flow programme in the UK, which is developing end-to-end systems and processes for managing and preserving born-digital electronic records,[8] the e-Depot programme at the Koninklijke Bibliotheek (the National Library of the Netherlands),[9] the Public Record Office of Victoria's VERS programme,[10] and the National Archives of Australia's digital preservation programme.[11]

International collaboration

It has long been recognized that the challenges of digital preservation are too large and diverse to be resolved by any single organization, and that collaboration at all levels is essential. There are two main mechanisms by which such collaboration is enabled.

Fora

A variety of temporary or permanent fora exist to support collaboration and enable like-minded organizations to work together. Examples of such fora, which are significant in the areas of digital preservation and management, are described in this section.

The Digital Preservation Coalition (DPC) was established in 2001 to foster and co-ordinate collaborative action to address the challenges of preserving digital resources in the UK.[12] It currently has 26 members drawn from a wide range of organizations within the UK and beyond. Its advocacy campaign has been instrumental in raising the profile of digital preservation in the UK, and provides an effective means of reaching key stakeholders in funding bodies, government and industry. The DPC commissions and publishes a range of reports on significant topics, including the influential handbook *Preservation Management of Digital Materials* (Beagrie and Jones, 2001),[13] and a series of 'Technology Watch' reports. It hosts regular meetings and fora to address particular themes in digital preservation, and also sponsors the prestigious Digital Preservation Award, held every 18 months, which attracts a wide variety of international entries. The DPC is widely seen as a model for collaborative national activity.

The DLM-Forum was established by the European Commission in 1999, to co-ordinate archives, records and document lifecycle management activities across Europe. It has a membership of over 35 national archives, universities and suppliers. Its single most significant achievement has been the development of the MoReq (Model Requirements for the Management of Electronic Records) standard,[14] which established a common set of functional requirements for electronic records management systems. A revised version, MoReq2, is now under development, which will include requirements for long-term preservation.

The International Internet Preservation Consortium (IIPC) is a major focus of international collaboration over web archiving, and has already been described in detail in Chapter 2, The Development of Web Archiving.

The RLG (formerly the Research Libraries Group) is a non-profit organization which works 'to increase online discovery and delivery of research resources, enable global resource sharing, and foster digital preservation for long-term access'.[15] It has a global membership of over 150 libraries, archives, and museums, and has undertaken a number of significant projects in the field of digital preservation, including the development of a certification scheme for trusted digital repositories (in conjunction with the National Archives and Records Administration in the United States),[16] and PREMIS, a standard for preservation metadata (in conjunction with the Online Computer Library Center).[17]

Projects

Much important work in the field of digital preservation is undertaken through funded projects, at a national and international level. For example, in the UK the Joint Information Systems Committee (JISC) of the Higher Education Funding Councils for England is a major funder of digital preservation research. Perhaps its single most significant project to date has been the establishment of the Digital Curation Centre (DCC), which has been established to support digital curation within the UK academic research community.[18] The DCC was established in 2004, with initial funding for three years, by a consortium which comprises the universities of Edinburgh and Glasgow, UKOLN at the University of Bath and the Council for the Central Research Laboratory of the Research Councils. Although its primary remit is academic research data, the DCC is also working to support digital preservation more widely.

At a European level, significant funding is made available under the European Union's Research Framework Programmes. The Sixth Framework Programme (FP6) was established in 2003 with a total budget of €17.5 billion, to foster better use of European research efforts through the creation of a European Research Area. Within the thematic area of 'Information Society Technologies', which has been allocated €3.6 billion, a number of important digital preservation projects have been funded, including:

1   DELOS Network of Excellence on Digital Libraries: The DELOS network was established in 2004 to co-ordinate research into building digital libraries, and includes preservation as a major research topic.[19]
2   PrestoSPACE: The PrestoSPACE consortium comprises over 30 archival institutions, research bodies, universities and commercial partners, and was established to develop preservation services for audio-visual materials.[20]

FP6 will continue to run until the end of 2006, and is likely to fund further preservation projects in future. The Seventh Framework Programme, which is scheduled to run between 2007 and 2013, will provide an estimated €72 billion of further funding, and may be expected to promote further significant research into the management and preservation of digital resources.

International standards

A number of international standards have been developed which address aspects of digital preservation.

Standards governing the creation and management of information by data creators are an essential prerequisite for preservation. Two key sets of international standards exist in the area of records management. ISO 15489-1/2: 2001 sets standards for records management practice, while ISO 23081-1: 2006 establishes standards for records management metadata.

The major standard defining the fundamental requirements for a digital preservation system is the Open Archival Information Systems (OAIS) reference model (described in Chapter 6, Preservation). This has been ratified as an international standard (ISO 14721: 2003), and its terminology and concepts are now widely adopted. It forms the basis for the certification scheme for trusted digital repositories referred to in the previous section.

Increasing recognition of the need for open standards for digital object formats has begun to be reflected in the formal standards arena. The PDF/A standard (ISO 19005-1: 2005) defines a constrained subset of the Portable Document Format (PDF) specification, which is designed to maximize long-term accessibility. Based on PDF version 1.4, PDF/A maximizes the self-containment, platform independence and level of self-description of PDF files, by forbidding the use of certain features and mandating how other features may be used.

In 2005, Microsoft submitted its new XML-based Office 12 formats to Ecma International, a European standards body, and has stated that it intends to pursue their adoption as ISO standards. In a similar vein, the OpenDocument format used in alternative office software suites such as OpenOffice has been adopted as a standard by OASIS, the Organization for the Advancement of Structured Information Standards.[21] OASIS has already submitted the OpenDocument format to ISO/IEC JTC1, the ISO International Electrotechnical Commission's Joint Technical Committee, for ratification as a *de jure* standard.

From the web archiving perspective, it is also significant that the core technologies of the world wide web, such as HTML and XML, are defined as internationally recognized standards, in the form of W3C recommendations.[22]

Future tools

It is expected that future research will result in an increasing number of practical tools and services to support operational digital preservation programmes. New tools and techniques may be expected in the following areas:

- sophisticated tools to characterize digital objects, enabling an increasingly rich set of properties to be automatically captured; new techniques for semantic analysis and automatic classification of content may allow much cataloguing to be performed automatically
- support for rigorous preservation planning, including online technology watch services and advanced risk assessment methodologies
- the emergence of a global network of registries to support long-term preservation; such registries are likely to focus on file formats in the first instance, but should expand to cover the full range of representation information, and to support automation of the development and execution of preservation plans
- archival-quality migration tools, and international benchmarking of tried-and-tested migration pathways for common file formats
- improved emulation tools, and a better understanding of their viability and role as part of a comprehensive preservation toolkit
- the development of new preservation strategies designed both to meet the challenges of, and take advantage of, developing information technologies.

Web archiving tools

Initiatives such as the IIPC Toolkit (see Chapter 2, The Development of Web Archiving) illustrate a growing maturity in the development of web archiving tools. The combination of collaboration between the leading innovators in the field, international agreement on standards supporting interoperability and the release of tools under open-source licences, which both maximizes their availability and supports ongoing collaborative development, provides grounds for optimism. If the IIPC can maintain its current pace of development, and successfully extend its remit to address the broadest constituency of web archiving organizations, then there is every reason to expect that a well-integrated set of solutions for website collection and delivery will be available in the near future.

Developments which may be anticipated over the next few years are likely to include:

- 'smarter' web crawlers, which can autonomously identify content for collection within defined selection parameters and perform continuous crawling with limited manual intervention
- improved tools for collecting dynamic content and the deep web
- workflow systems to support and automate the entire web archiving process, from selection and collection through quality assurance to storage and delivery
- more sophisticated delivery systems, providing improved searching, more authentic and functional recreation of dynamic content and improved support for the reuse of archived data.

Web technology

The pace of innovation in web technology shows no sign of abating. Although recent years have been characterized by evolutionary developments, there are indications that more fundamental changes may occur in the near future.

Web 2.0, the Semantic Web and beyond

The term 'Web 2.0' has been coined to describe the increasingly dynamic nature of the web that we are seeing today, and which will become increasingly prevalent in the near future. In this context, the original world wide web, comprising simple, static documents, is retrospectively referred to as 'Web 1.0'. The user experience of Web 1.0 was essentially passive, navigating and viewing a set of predefined, dumb web pages. Web 2.0 is characterized by its much more interactive nature, and sophisticated capabilities for describing and discovering online resources. Users now have much more direct input: not only can content be dynamically generated in response to their requests but, through technologies such as blogs and wikis, those same users can create and change content in an online environment. The web has moved from a 'read-only' to a 'read/write' environment.

The Semantic Web is closely linked to notions of Web 2.0. The Semantic Web is a project directed by Tim Berners-Lee, which aims to extend the world wide web into a universal medium for exchanging information, by applying machine-interpretable meaning, or semantics, to web content. It uses a number of standards and technologies to express descriptive and structural information about the content of web documents, to support advanced, automated searching and analysis of online information. These enabling technologies include XML, the Resource Description Framework (RDF) and the Web Ontology Language (OWL). RDF is a metadata model which provides a means to encode descriptions of resources which can then be interpreted by software, and OWL is an example of one of the vocabularies which can be used to formulate these descriptions. These technologies already underpin much active research in the e-science domain, such as the myGrid project.[23]

There is already considerable debate about the likely shape of 'Web 3.0': it is anticipated that this will bring a much more decentralized, collaborative web, which will effectively provide a web-based operating system. In this scenario, it is likely that the boundary between the desktop and the online world will become blurred to the point of invisibility, with users storing their data on web servers and manipulating it using web-based applications. Web 3.0 may well provide a single, immersive 'metaverse', a virtual online environment which seamlessly supports the interactions between users, applications and data.

Conclusion

The challenges that this will pose for those wishing to preserve web content are difficult to predict. However, it is certain that the increasingly dynamic and customizable nature of the web will render the notion of fixed content, which can be discretely, objectively identified and archived, ever more obsolete. Although the technical obstacles are likely to be surmountable with 'smarter', more autonomous web harvesters, and increasingly transactional collection methods, it is the cultural shift that will be required of collecting organizations, in order to transform their curatorial traditions in the face of such a radically different cultural landscape, which may prove to be the greatest challenge.

However, if the world wide web is to achieve its transformation to a comprehensive environment for knowledge sharing and interaction, supporting a fully-fledged global knowledge economy, it is paramount that the information it contains is sustainable and reliable. The techniques of web archiving provide the beginnings of a means to achieve that goal. The sophistication of these techniques will need to grow in step with the web itself. In the future, web archiving will itself need to transform into 'web information management', a comprehensive approach to managing and sustaining the information assets that form the very essence of the world wide web.

Notes and references

1   See www.zurich.ibm.com/st/storage/concept.html [accessed 19 February 2006].

2   See http://lcg.web.cern.ch/lcg/ [accessed 19 February 2006].

3   See www.ecmwf.int/services/computing/overview/datahandling.html [accessed 19 February 2006].

4   Fusco, L., Guidetti, V. and van Bemmelen, J. (2005) e-Collaboration and Grid-on-Demand Computing for Earth Science at ESA, *ERCIM News*, **61**, www.ercim.org/publication/ercim_news/enw61/fusco.html [accessed 19 February 2006].

5   Hey, T. and Trefethen, A. (2003) The Data Deluge: an e-science perspective. In Berman, F., Fox, G. and Hey, T. (eds) *Grid Computing: making the global infrastructure a reality*, Wiley, www.rcuk.ac.uk/escience/documents/report_datadeluge.pdf [accessed 18 February 2006].

6   See www.digitalpreservation.gov/ [accessed 19 February 2006].

7   See www.archives.gov/era [accessed 19 February 2006].

8   See www.nationalarchives.gov.uk/electronicrecords/seamless_flow/ [accessed 19 February 2006].

9   See www.kb.nl/dnp/e-depot/e-depot-en.html [accessed 19 February 2006].

10 See www.prov.vic.gov.au/vers/vers/default.htm [accessed 19 February 2006].

11 See www.naa.gov.au/recordkeeping/preservation/digital/summary.html [accessed 19 February 2006].

12 See www.dpconline.org/ [accessed 19 February 2006].

13 Beagrie, N. and Jones, M. (2001) *Preservation Management of Digital Materials: a handbook*, London, The British Library, www.dpconline.org.graphics/handbook [accessed 1 April 2006].

14 European Commission (2001) *Model Requirements for the Management of Electronic Records: MoReq specification*, INSAR Supplement **VI**, European Commission, http://europa.eu.int/idabc/en/document/2631/5585 [accessed 20 November 2005].

15 From the RLG mission statement. See www.rlg.org/en/page.php?page_id=362 [accessed 19 February 2006].

16 See www.rlg.org/en/page.php?Page_ID=583 [accessed 19 February 2006].

17 See www.rlg.org/en/page.php?page_id=7821 [accessed 19 February 2006].

18 See www.dcc.ac.uk/ [accessed 19 February 2006].

19 See www.delos.info/ [accessed 19 February 2006].

20 See www.prestospace.org/ [accessed 19 February 2006].

21 Organization for the Advancement of Structured Information Standards (2005) *Open Document Format for Office Applications (OpenDocument) v1.0*, OASIS Standard, 2005, www.oasis-open.org/committees/download.php/12572/opendocument-v1.0-os.pdf [accessed 18 February 2006].

22 See www.w3.org/tr/ [accessed 19 February 2006].

23 See www.mygrid.org.uk/ [accessed 19 February 2006].

Appendix 1

Web archiving and preservation tools

This appendix lists the main software tools described in the text. Each tool is classified according to its basic type. The type of licence under which the software is available is described, if applicable, together with URLs for websites that contain further information. A URL is also given if the software is freely available to download.

BnFArcTools (BAT)
Type: ARC file manipulation tool
Licence: GNU General Public License
Information: http://bibnum.bnf.fr/downloads/bat/
Download: http://bibnum.bnf.fr/downloads/bat/

CERN Advanced Storage Manager (CASTOR)
Type: Storage management system
Licence: GNU General Public License
Information: http://castor.web.cern.ch/castor/
Download: http://castor.web.cern.ch/castor/

DeepArc
Type: Database archiving tool
Licence: GNU General Public License
Information: http://deeparc.sourceforge.net/
Download: http://sourceforge.net/projects/deeparc/

DROID
Type: Automatic file format identification tool
Licence: Berkeley Software Distribution license
Information: www.nationalarchives.gov.uk/aboutapps/pronom/droid.htm
Download: www.nationalarchives.gov.uk/aboutapps/pronom/droid.htm

DSpace
Type: Repository system
Licence: Berkeley Software Distribution License
Information: www.dspace.org/
Download: http://sourceforge.net/projects/dspace/

EPrints
Type: Repository system
Licence: GNU General Public License
Information: www.eprints.org/
Download: www.eprints.org/

Fedora
Type: Repository system
Licence: Educational Community License
Information: www.fedora.info/
Download: www.fedora.info/

Heritrix
Type: Web crawler
Licence: GNU Lesser General Public License
Information: http://sourceforge.net/projects/archive-crawler/
Download: http://sourceforge.net/projects/archive-crawler/

HTTrack
Type: Web crawler
Licence: GNU General Public License
Information: www.httrack.com
Download: www.httrack.com

JHOVE
Type: Format validation tool
Licence: GNU Lesser General Public License
Information: http://hul.harvard.edu/jhove/
Download: http://hul.harvard.edu/jhove/

LOCKSS
Type: Repository system
Licence: Berkeley Software Distribution License
Information: www.lockss.org/
Download: www.lockss.org/publicdocs/install.html

NLNZ metadata extractor
Type: Metadata extraction tool
Licence: NLNZ License
Information: www.natlib.govt.nz/en/whatsnew/4initiatives.
html#extraction
Download: www.natlib.govt.nz/en/whatsnew/4initiatives.html#extraction

NutchWAX
Type: Web archive search engine
Licence: GNU Lesser General Public License
Information: http://archive-access.sourceforge.net/projects/nutch/
Download: http://archive-access.sourceforge.net/projects/nutch/

PageVault
Type: Transactional archiving tool
Licence: Commercial license
Information: www.projectcomputing.com/products/pagevault/
Download: Not applicable

PANDAS
Type: Workflow and repository system
Licence: Not applicable
Information: http://pandora.nla.gov.au/pandas.html
Download: Not applicable

PRONOM
Type: Online technical registry
Licence: Not applicable
Information: www.nationalarchives.gov.uk/pronom/
Download: Not applicable – free online service

SIARD
Type: Database archiving tool
Licence: Not applicable
Information: www.bar.admin.ch/
Download: Not applicable

Storage Resource Broker (SRB)
Type: Storage management system
Licence: Commercial/Berkeley Software Distribution License – SRB is free
    to academic organizations and US government agencies. A commercial
    version is also available.
Information: www.sdsc.edu/srb/
Download: Dependent on status

Universal Virtual Computer for images
Type: Universal Virtual Computer proof-of-concept
Licence: IBM licence
Information: www.alphaworks.ibm.com/tech/uvc/
Download: www.alphaworks.ibm.com/tech/uvc/download/

W3C Validators
Type: Online validation service
Licence: Not applicable
Information: http://validator.w3.org/
Download: Not applicable – free online service

Wayback Machine
Type: Web archive access tool
Licence: GNU Lesser General Public License
Information: http://archive-access.sourceforge.net/projects/wayback/
Download: http://archive-access.sourceforge.net/projects/wayback/

WERA
Type: Web archive access tool
Licence: GNU General Public License
Information: http://archive-access.sourceforge.net/project/wera/
Download: http://archive-access.sourceforge.net/project/wera/

Xena
Type: Normalization and access tool
Licence: GNU General Public License
Information: http://xena.sourceforge.net/
Download: http://xena.sourceforge.net/

Xinq
Type: Web archive access tool
Licence: Apache Software License
Information: www.nla.gov.au/xinq/
Download: http://sourceforge.net/projects/xinq/

Appendix 2
Model permissions form

Introduction

This appendix reproduces the British Library's version of the copyright permission documents used by the UK Web Archiving Consortium, which are reproduced by permission of UKWAC and the British Library. They are intended to provide an example of the types of form required for securing permissions to archive web resources from website owners.

It comprises a covering letter to the website owner, the copyright licence form itself and a set of frequently asked questions.

Permissions letter

Dear Sir/Madam,

WEBSITE TITLE

The British Library is a founding member of the UK Web Archiving Consortium (www.webarchive.org.uk) consisting of the British Library, JISC (Joint Information Systems Committee), The National Archives, the National Library of Scotland, the National Library of Wales and the Wellcome Library. The Consortium is undertaking a two-year pilot project to determine the long-term feasibility of archiving selected websites.

The British Library would like to invite you to participate in this pilot project by archiving your website under the terms of the appended licence. We select sites to represent aspects of UK documentary heritage and, as a result, they will remain available to researchers in the future. If the pilot is successful the archived copy of your website will subsequently form part of our permanent collections.

There are some benefits to you as a website owner in having your publication archived by the Consortium. If you grant us a licence, the Consortium will aim to take the necessary preservation action to keep your publication accessible as hardware and software changes over time.

If you are not the sole copyright owner please pass this request on to the other copyright owners. If you give the British Library permission to copy and archive your website we will store its contents electronically on a server owned by the UK Web Archiving Consortium. We will also seek to take the necessary action to maintain its accessibility over time and ensure its future integrity. Permission to archive pertains only to the website specified in this e-mail.

Please note that the Consortium reserves the right to take down any material from the archived site which, in its reasonable opinion, either infringes copyright or any other intellectual property right or is likely to be illegal.

If you are happy for your site to be included in this web archive please complete the attached copyright licence form and return it to the address given below. For more information about copyright, the UK Web Archiving Consortium and how your archived website will be made available, please see the attached FAQ document.

Alternatively, if you require any additional information, please do not hesitate to contact me.

Yours sincerely,

UKWAC copyright licence

I/We the undersigned grant the British Library, on behalf of the UK Web Archiving Consortium, a licence to make any reproductions or communications of this website as are reasonably necessary to preserve it over time and to make it available to the public:

Title of website	
URL	

(Please feel free to change the title details as appropriate)

Third-party content: Is any content on this website
subject to copyright and/or the database right
held by another party?   Yes ☐   No ☐

Has their permission to copy this content
been granted?   Yes ☐   No ☐

Note that we will not be able to archive this website if you do not have the permission of all third parties.

Licence granted by:

Name: (block letters)

Position: Organization:

E-mail: Tel:

Any other information:

I confirm that I am authorized to grant this licence on behalf of all the owners of copyright in the website; I further warrant that nothing contained in this website infringes the copyright or other intellectual property rights of any third party.

Signature: Date:

It would also be beneficial to our project if you could answer the following questions:

Do you presently archive this website
yourself/yourselves?   Yes ☐   No ☐
Details

Would you allow the archived website to be used in any future publicity for the Web Archive?   Yes ☐   No ☐

Frequently asked questions
What is the UK Web Archiving Consortium (UKWAC)?

A number of major UK institutions have joined together to form a consortium (UKWAC) to share the costs, expertise and facilities required to archive selected websites for future access. The UK institutions that form the consortium believe that there is enough consistency in the business requirements of web archiving to create a joint project to share the operational environment for the web archiving process. For more information about UKWAC please point your browser at www.webarchive.org.uk/.

Institutions that form the UK Web Archiving Consortium are: the British Library, The National Archives, the Wellcome Library, the National Library of Scotland, the National Library of Wales/Llyfrgell Genedlaethol Cymru and The Joint Information Systems Committee (JISC).

How will the web archiving project work?

Each consortium member will select and 'capture' content relevant to its subject and/or domain. For example, the British Library will archive sites of research value reflecting national culture and events of historical importance. These could include web pages focusing on key events in national life, museum web pages, e-theses, selected blogs to support research material, and web-based literary and creative projects by British subjects.

Does this mean that UKWAC will take over hosting my website?

No, you will still be responsible for hosting and maintaining your live website, just as you do now.

Won't my users become confused between archived and live websites?

We do not believe so. The UK Web Archiving Consortium archive will be clearly marked as containing archived websites and links will be provided to your current live website. All users will benefit from having access to material that is no longer available on live websites. In addition, the archive is not indexed by search engines such as Google, so users of search engines will never be directed to an archived version of your site.

How does the archiving work?

UK Web Archiving Consortium uses software developed by the National Library of Australia and used to build their Pandora Archive - see http://pandora.nla.gov.au. This software is used to manage the process of gathering websites.

The software works in a similar way to a browser, in that it makes requests of a host for files. The software follows links within a site and gathers files it finds. It is capable of gathering database-driven sites such as PHP or ASP sites. We can't, however, gather the contents of databases - the so-called 'deep web' - such as library catalogues.

The software cannot gather any material that is protected behind a password, nor can it 'crack' or 'break' passwords.

What am I doing when I grant the British Library a copyright licence?

When you grant the British Library a copyright licence, you are permitting it to make a copy of your website, to store it and to make it accessible to the public for the duration of the project in an archive of websites held on a server owned by the UK Web Archiving Consortium. If the project is successful, you are also permitting us to take the necessary steps to preserve your website as part of the Library's permanent collections and to make it accessible to the public now and in the future through a server hosted by the Library. This process might include the copying of files to different formats so that they remain accessible as hardware and software change in the future.

What is this licence?

In accordance with the Copyright, Designs and Patents Act 1988 permission to copy a publication (which includes websites) must be obtained from the publisher/author. As the British Library wants to copy a substantial portion of your website, we must seek your permission. 'Granting a licence' is the legal term for giving permission to copy a publication. The licence consists of the letter sent to you requesting that you grant the British Library a copyright licence and, if you agree to grant it, your returned signed copyright licence.

Am I giving away copyright in my website?

No. You still retain full copyright in your website, in both the live version of your website and the archived version in the Consortium's archive. If any third party wanted to copy more than an insubstantial portion (as defined by the Copyright, Designs and Patents Act 1988) either from the live version of your website or from the archived version, they would still be obliged to seek your permission.

Is the UKWAC archive run on a commercial basis?

No. Access to all websites in the UKWAC archive will be free of charge, and there is no charge for having your website in the UKWAC archive.

My site links to websites belonging to other organizations: will those sites be archived along with mine?

No, they won't. Links to sites that are external to your own will not be archived.

My site has a private area accessible only with a user ID and password: will this be archived?

No. Usually, secured areas like these will not be archived. You may, however, choose to give UKWAC a user ID and password and to allow archiving of these areas. Please feel free to discuss this with us.

How often will my website be archived?

A decision will be made on the frequency of capture desirable for each website based on the publication pattern, the importance of the information and the stability of the site.

How will my archived website be displayed?

For an example of how the web archive may be presented on the web, please point your browser at: http://pandora.nla.gov.au/index.html. When the version of your website in the archive is accessed, a title entry page will display first. This will provide introductory information about the title, including a link to your live site, a general statement about copyright and a link to your own copyright statement if such a statement is provided. If access to a website needs to be restricted for some reason (for instance, if it is a commercial title or the contents are culturally sensitive) the necessary protective measures can also be put in place. We are happy to discuss this with all copyright owners.

I produce a website: can I suggest it for inclusion in the UKWAC archive?

Yes. We'll be pleased to hear suggestions from you. We won't necessarily accept every suggested website for archiving but we'd still be pleased to hear about your site.

Can I suggest websites produced by other organizations or people?

You could, but we need to get permission from the creators or publishers of those websites before we can archive them.

Appendix 3

Model test script

This appendix provides a model test script for use in the quality assurance process. It is based on the test script in use by The National Archives of the UK, and is intended for testing remotely harvested content, using a sampling approach to quality assurance. However, it could be easily adapted to other circumstances.

The script comprises two parts: the test script guidelines, which describe how the test is to be performed, and the test script pro-forma, which is completed by the tester as a record of each test.

Test script guidelines
Introduction
This is the test script for the UK Government Web Archive. It is to be completed by nominated staff within The National Archives only.

Objective
To ensure that the website and all content within the website has been captured correctly.

Testing guidelines
1   Before tests are carried out, please complete the following in the script:

Name: The name of the tester.

Department: The government department that maintains the website being tested.

Test date: The date on which the test was performed.

Website name: The name of the website being tested, as described in the TNA catalogue.

2   Open Internet Explorer and type in the following URL to invoke The National Archives web archiving system: www.nationalarchives. gov.uk/ preservation/webarchive/.

3   Enter the URL for the website to be tested in the search box and click 'Search'. This will invoke an index of available snapshots. Record the original URL under 'Original URL' in the script.

4   Select from the index the snapshot to be tested – this will open the snapshot. Record the date of the snapshot under 'Crawl date' in the script.

5   Follow steps 1–11 of the script. Tick the Pass/Fail/Not applicable boxes as appropriate, followed by any additional observations in the Comments section. You may wish to open the live version of the website in a new browser window, for comparative purposes. Note that this is to be used only as a reference and it may not be directly comparable owing to differences in date.

6   Log any issues identified which require resolution in the Issues Log.

Notes on test steps

1   This test is automatically passed if the snapshot can be invoked.

2   Test a representative sample of all appropriate navigation methods, including menu bars, side bars and in-text links. Test navigation to at least two levels below the homepage.

4–8   Test a representative sample of each content type. Ensure that all tested content is being delivered from the archive rather than the live website.

9–10   Test a representative selection of search terms.

Test script pro-forma

Name:

Department:

Test date:

Website name:

Original URL:

Crawl date:

Step	Test description	Pass	Fail	N/A	Comments
1	Is the site available?				
2	Does site navigation function correctly? (Test at least 2 levels below the home page)				
3	Does the site display the correct archived date?				
4	Are frames displayed correctly?				
5	Has the text been captured correctly?				
6	Have images been captured correctly?				
7	Has multimedia content been captured correctly? (e.g. Flash)				
8	Can files be downloaded?				
9	Does the search function work?				
10	Does the search function retrieve the correct web pages?				
11	Other issues identified				

Appendix 4

Model issues log

This appendix provides a model issues log (overleaf) to be used for recording any issues identified during the quality assurance testing process that require resolution. It is based on the issues log in use by The National Archives of the UK.

Issue ID	Date identified	Identified by	Website name	Test date	Affected URL	Description	Status	Priority	Date reported	Resolution	Date closed

Appendix 5
Model job description

Introduction

This appendix provides a sample job description for a generic web archivist. The envisaged role is technically oriented, such as might be required to implement a web archiving programme within an organization that has existing curatorial expertise. If required, this role could be divided into a number of more specialized posts.

Web archivist job description
Job purpose

As part of our developing web archiving programme, you will be responsible for the administration of two ongoing projects:

1   A contracted-out web harvesting programme for the repeated harvesting of selected websites. You will liaise with the contractor to ensure that websites are harvested in accordance with the specified collection list, perform quality assurance on the harvested websites, and liaise with the contractor to resolve any identified issues.
2   A collaborative programme with a consortium of partner organizations. You will undertake the collection, quality assurance and cataloguing

of websites using the consortium's shared infrastructure, and liaise with other consortium members and with IT system suppliers.

You will also contribute to developing supporting technologies and standards for digital preservation of websites. Suitable candidates must be team players, enthusiastic to help take us forward into an exciting new era.

Main responsibilities

The main responsibilities of the role are:

- initiation, configuring and monitoring of harvests
- cataloguing of websites to designated standards
- quality assurance of collected websites
- resolution of identified quality issues
- liaison with relevant internal departments, e.g. those responsible for selection of websites and online delivery
- liaison with external parties, e.g. third party suppliers, website owners and relevant external initiatives
- assistance with the administration, support and maintenance of IT systems, including web crawling applications and data storage systems
- working with the digital preservation team to develop and enhance innovative methodologies, techniques and tools to support web archiving and long-term preservation.

Work experience and technical competence
Essential
The following are considered essential:

- graduate level qualification in an information science or computing-related subject
- knowledge of web technologies and utilities, including:
  - mark-up languages such as HTML and XHTML
  - scripting languages such as JavaScript and Perl
  - dynamic web technologies such as ASP
- strong oral and written communication skills

- ability to work productively as part of a team
- ability to work under pressure to achieve targets
- a willingness to keep up to date with innovations in web archiving and digital preservation and to develop your professional skills.

Desirable

The following skills and experience are considered desirable:

- experience of using open-source software
- knowledge of web standards, e.g. accessibility standards, and mark-up language standards
- understanding of library and/or archive cataloguing systems
- understanding of the principles of long-term preservation of complex data.

Bibliography

Cm 4310 (1999) *Modernising Government: Presented to Parliament by the Prime Minister and the Minister for the Cabinet Office by Command of Her Majesty*, The Stationery Office, www.archive.official-documents.co.uk/document/cm43/4310/4310.htm [accessed 29 October 2005].

ISO 14721: 2003. *Space data and information transfer systems – Open archival information system – Reference model.*

ISO 19005-1: 2005. *Document management – Electronic document file format for long-term preservation – Part 1: Use of PDF 1.4 (PDF/A-1).*

ISO 15489-1: 2001. *Information and documentation – Records management – Part 1: General.*

ISO 15489-2: 2001. *Information and documentation – Records management – Part 2: Guidelines.*

ISO 23081-1: 2006. *Information and documentation – Records management processes – Metadata for records – Part 1: Principles.*

Adobe Systems Incorporated (1992) *TIFF Revision 6.0,* http://partners.adobe.com/public/developer/en/tiff/TIFF6.pdf [accessed 28 October 2005].

Beagrie, N. and Jones, M. (2001) *Preservation Management of Digital Materials: a handbook*, London, The British Library, www.dpconline.org.graphics/handbook [accessed 1 April 2006].

Beedham, H., Missen, J., Palmer, M. and Ruusalepp, R. (2005) *Assessment of UKDA and TNA Compliance with OAIS and METS Standards*, UK Data Archive, University of Essex, www.data-archive.ac.uk/news/publications/oaismets.pdf [accessed 18 February 2006].

Bergman, M. K. (2001) The Deep Web: surfacing hidden value, *Journal of Electronic Publishing*, **7** (1), www.press.umich.edu/jep/07-01/bergman.html [accessed 23 November 2004].

Borrull, A. L. and Oppenheim, C. (2004) Legal aspects of the Web, *Annual Review of Information Science and Technology*, **38**, 483–548.

Brown, A. (2003) Selecting Storage Media for Long-term Preservation, *Digital Preservation Guidance Note*, **2**, London, The National Archives, www.nationalarchives.gov.uk/preservation/advice/pdf/selecting_storage_media.pdf [accessed 23 October 2005].

Brown, A. (2005) The PRONOM PUID Scheme: a scheme of persistent unique identifiers for representation information, *Digital Preservation Technical Paper*, **2**, London, The National Archives, www.nationalarchives.gov.uk/aboutapps/pronom/pdf/pronom_unique_identifier_scheme.pdf [accessed 19 February 2006].

Brown, A. (forthcoming) Multiple Manifestations: managing change in a digital preservation environment, *Digital Preservation Technical Paper*, **3**, London, The National Archives.

Charlesworth, A. (2003) *Legal Issues Relating to the Archiving of Internet Resources in the UK, EU, USA and Australia: a study undertaken for the JISC and the Wellcome Trust*, University of Bristol, www.jisc.ac.uk/uploaded_documents/archiving_legal.pdf [accessed 19 February 2006].

Christensen-Dalsgaard, B., Fønss-Jørgensen, E., von Hielmcrone, H., Finneman, N. O., Brügger, N., Henriksen, B. and Carlsen, S. V. (2003) *Experiences and Conclusions from a Pilot Study: web archiving of the district and county elections 2001 – final report for the pilot project 'netarkivet.dk' (English version)*, Statsbiblioteket and Kongelige Bibliotek, Denmark, http://netarkivet.dk/rap/webark-final-rapport-2003.pdf [accessed 18 February 2006].

Day, M. (2003) *Collecting and Preserving the World Wide Web: a feasibility study undertaken for the JISC and Wellcome Trust*, JISC and Wellcome Trust, http://library.welcome.ac.uk/assets/wtl039229.pdf [accessed 23 October 2005].

Eastlake, D. (2001) *RFC 3171: US secure hash algorithm (SHA-1)*, Internet Engineering Task Force, www.ietf.org/rfc/rfc3174.txt [accessed 18 February 2006].

European Commission (2001) *Model Requirements for the Management of Electronic Records: MoReq specification*, INSAR Supplement **VI**, European Commission, http://europa.eu.int/idabc/en/document/2631/5585 [accessed 20 November 2005].

Fitch, K. (2003) *Website Archiving: an approach to recording every materially different response produced by a website*, Project Computing, http://ausweb.scu.edu.au/aw03/papers/fitch/ [accessed 19 February 2006].

Fusco, L., Guidetti, V. and van Bemmelen, J. (2005) e-Collaboration and Grid-on-Demand Computing for Earth Science at ESA, *ERCIM News*, **61**, www.ercim.org/publication/ercim_news/enw61/fusco.html [accessed 19 February 2006].

Garrett, J. and Waters, D. (eds) (1996) *Preserving Digital Information: report of the Task Force on Archiving of Digital Information*, Commission on Preservation and Access and The Research Libraries Group, www.rlg.org/legacy/ftpd/pub/archtf/final-report.pdf [accessed 19 February 2006].

Great Britain, Department for Constitutional Affairs (2002) *Lord Chancellor's Code of Practice on the Management of Records. Issued under section 46 of the Freedom of Information Act 2000.*

Great Britain, Department for Constitutional Affairs (2004) *Secretary of State for Constitutional Affairs' Code of Practice on the Discharge of Public Authorities' Functions under Part I of the Freedom of Information Act 2000. Issued under section 45 of the Act.*

Heslop, H., Davis, S. and Wilson, A. (2002) *An Approach to the Preservation of Digital Records*, National Archives of Australia, www.naa.gov.au/recordkeeping/er/digital_preservation/green_paper.pdf [accessed 28 October 2005].

Hey, T. and Trefethen, A. (2003) The Data Deluge: an e-science perspective. In Berman, F., Fox, G. and Hey, T. (eds) *Grid Computing: making the global infrastructure a reality*, Wiley, www.rcuk.ac.uk/escience/documents/report_datadeluge.pdf [accessed 18 February 2006].

International Council on Archives (ICA) (2000) *ISAD(G): General International Standard Archival Description*, 2nd edn.

Koehler, W. (2004) A Longitudinal Study of Web Pages Continued: a consideration of document persistence, *Information Research*, **9** (2), http://informationr.net/ir/9-2/paper174.html [accessed 16 February 2006].

Lawrence, G. W., Kehoe, W. R., Rieger, O. Y., Walters, W. H., and Kenney, A. R. (2000) *Risk Management of Digital Information: a file format investigation*, Council on Library and Information Resources, www.clir.org/pubs/abstract/pub93abst.html [accessed 28 October 2005].

Lorie, R. A. (2002) The UVC: a method for preserving digital documents – proof of concept, *IBM/KB Long-term Preservation Study Report Series*, IBM Global Services.

Lyman, P. (2002) Archiving the World Wide Web. In *Building a National Strategy for Digital Preservation: issues in digital media archiving*, Council on Library and Information Resources Report, **106**, 38–51, www.clir.org/pubs/reports/pub106/pub106.pdf [accessed 23 November 2004].

Mohr, G., Stack, M., Ranitovic, I., Avery, D. and Kimpton, M. (2004) *An Introduction to Heritrix: an open source archival quality web crawler,*

The Internet Archive,
www.crawler.archive.org/an%20introduction%20to%20heritrix.pdf
[accessed 1 November 2005].

Office of the e-Envoy (2003) *Guidelines for UK Government Websites: illustrated handbook for web management teams*, The Stationery Office,
www.cabinetoffice.gov.uk/e-government/resources/handbook/introduction.asp [accessed 19 February 2006].

Organization for the Advancement of Structured Information Standards (2005) *Open Document Format for Office Applications (OpenDocument) v1.0*, OASIS Standard, 2005,
www.oasis-open.org/committees/download.php/12572/opendocument-v1.0-os.pdf [accessed 18 February 2006].

Padfield, T. (2004) *Copyright for Archivists and Users of Archives*, 2nd edn, Facet Publishing.

PREMIS Working Group (2005) *Data Dictionary for Preservation Metadata: Final Report of the PREMIS Working Group*, RLG and Online Computer Library Center (OCLC),
www.oclc.org/research/projects/pmwg/premis-final.pdf [accessed 19 February 2006].

Rauch, C. and Rauber, A. (2004) *Towards an Analytical Evaluation of Preservation Strategies: presentation for the ERPANET workshop, 10–11 May 2004, Vienna*, Technische Universität Wien,
www.erpanet.org/events/2004/vienna/presentations/erpatrainingvienna_rauber.pdf [accessed 28 October 2005].

RLG (2005) *An Audit Checklist for the Certification of Trusted Digital Repositories*, RLG and National Archives and Records Administration,
www.rlg.org/en/pdfs/rlgnara-repositorieschecklist.pdf [accessed 23 October 2005].

Rivest, R. (1992) *RFC 1321: the MD5 message-digest algorithm*, Internet Engineering Task Force,
www.ietf.org/rfc/rfc1321.txt [accessed 18 February 2006].

Rosenthal, D. S. H., Lipkis, T., Robertson, T. S. and Morabito, S. (2005)

Transparent Format Migration of Preserved Web Content, *D-Lib Magazine*, **11** (1), www.dlib.org/dlib/january05/rosenthal/ 01rosenthal.html [accessed 28 October 2005].

Rothenberg, J. (1999) *Avoiding Technological Quicksand: finding a viable technical foundation for digital preservation. A report to the Council on Library and Information Resources*, Council on Library and Information Resources, www.clir.org/pubs/abstract/pub77.html [accessed 28 October 2005].

Slats, J. (ed.) (2003) *Digital Preservation Testbed White Paper: emulation: context and current status*, ICTU, www.digitaleduurzaamheid.nl/bibliotheek/docs/white_paper_emulatie_en.pdf [accessed 31 October 2005].

Stanescu, A. (2004) Assessing the Durability of Formats in a Digital Preservation Environment: the INFORM methodology, *D-Lib Magazine*, **10** (11), www.dlib.org/dlib/november04/stanescu/ 11stanescu.html [accessed 19 February 2006].

The National Archives (2003) *Operational Selection Policy 27: the selection of government websites*, www.nationalarchives.gov.uk/recordsmanagement/selection/pdf/osp27.pdf [accessed 29 October 2005].

Thelwall, M., Vaughan, L. and Björneborn, L. (2005) Webometrics, *Annual Review of Information Science and Technology*, **39**, 81–135.

Index

Also from Facet Publishing

Digital Preservation

Marilyn Deegan, Director of Research Development, Centre for Computing in the Humanities, King's College London
Simon Tanner, Director, KCL Digital Consultancy Services, King's College London (editors)

Digital preservation is an issue of huge importance to the library and information profession right now. Digital data is being produced on a massive scale by individuals and institutions: some of it is born, lives and dies only in digital form, and it is the potential death of this data that is the concern of this book.

Each chapter is written by an international expert on the topic, with case studies and examples used to ground ideas and theories in real concerns and practice. The book will arm the information professional with the knowledge they need about this important and pressing issue and give examples of best practice to help find a way to a solution for this problem. Chapters include:

- the key issues in digital preservation
- strategies for digital preservation
- the status of preservation metadata in the digital library community
- web archiving
- the costs of digital preservation
- it's money that matters in long-term digital preservation
- some European approaches to digital preservation.

This is an indispensable guide for all information managers, librarians and archivists. Others in the information and culture world, such as museum curators, media professionals and web content providers will also find it essential reading, as will students of digital culture on library and information studies and other courses.

Digital Futures Series
Series editors Marilyn Deegan and Simon Tanner

September 2006; 256pp; hardback; 1-85604-485-8; £39.95

Ethics, Accountability, and Recordkeeping in a Dangerous World

Richard J. Cox, Professor in Library and Information Science at the School of Information Sciences, University of Pittsburgh

The new book from this eminent American archivist covers a wide range of recent issues and controversies related to the mission and work of archivists and records managers. The essays contained in it consider both the practical issues of administering records and the much more contentious issues related to public policy and recordkeeping. The book is intended to push both archivists and records managers to reconsider their notions of the ethical dimension of their work and how they define their societal and organizational priorities.

This significant text will challenge archivists and records managers to re-think their own perspectives about such matters, asking if their professional associations' ethics codes are sufficient, given recent challenges to the control of records and information in government agencies, corporations, and even cultural institutions. Key topics include:

- from accountability to ethics, or when do records professionals become whistleblowers?
- testing the spirit of the information age
- searching for authority and recognition: archivists, records managers and electronic records
- the world is a dangerous place: recordkeeping in the age of terror
- technology, the future of work, and records professionals
- records and truth in the post-truth society
- censorship and records
- archiving archives: rethinking and revitalizing a concept.

With a foreword by Sarah Tyacke, former Chief Executive of The National Archives, this important debate will be of great interest to records professionals and archivists worldwide needing to know how the issues will impinge on their work.

**Principles and Practice in Records Management and Archives Series
Series editor Geoffrey Yeo**

September 2006; 256pp; hardback; 1-85604-596-X; £44.95

Preserving Archives

Helen Forde, independent consultant on archives

Access to archival material is dependent on the survival of fragile materials: paper, parchment, photographic materials, audiovisual materials and, most recently, magnetic and optical formats. The primary importance of such survival is widely acknowledged but sometimes overlooked in a rush to provide ever better means of access.

Archivists in all types of organizations face questions of how to plan a preservation strategy in less than perfect circumstances, or deal with a sudden emergency. This book considers the causes of threats to the basic material, outlines the preservation options available and offers flexible solutions applicable in a variety of situations. Benefiting from the author's contact with international specialists as Head of Preservation Services at The National Archives of the UK, it offers a wide range of case studies and examples. Key topics are:

- standards and policies of archive preservation
- preservation assessment
- understanding archive materials and their characteristics
- managing digital preservation
- archive buildings and their characteristics
- managing archival storage
- managing risks and avoiding disaster
- setting up a conservation workshop
- handling and moving records
- exhibiting archives
- managing a pest control programme
- using and creating surrogates.

This is a vital handbook for professional archivists, but also for the many librarians, curators and enthusiasts, trained and untrained, in museums, local studies centres and voluntary societies in need of good clear advice.

Principles and Practice in Records Management and Archives Series Series editor Geoffrey Yeo

December 2006; 224pp; hardback; 1-85604-577-3; £39.95

Management Skills for Archivists and Records Managers

Elizabeth Shepherd, Senior Lecturer in Archives and Records Management at the School of Library, Archive and Information Studies, University College London
Karen Anderson, Senior Lecturer at the School of Computer and Information Science, Edith Cowan University, Australia

This book introduces the range of management skills employed by records managers and archivists, and shows how they may be applied, adding value both in terms of personal professional development and in the organizational benefits of service delivery, excellence, accountability and transparency in both large and small archive and records management units.

Each chapter deals with a key aspect of archive and records management, illustrated by case studies and examples. Throughout, the book provides a clear conceptual framework, but ensures that this is translated into practical terms to enable the reader to make use of the knowledge in their work. The chapters are:

- identifying management skills for archivists and records managers
- taking the long term view: corporate and strategic planning
- managing projects successfully
- managing money and other resources
- managing people
- providing accountability: performance measurement
- advocating for archives and records management
- developing personal management skills.

The book is a key resource for records managers and archivists working in any sector, especially those at the start of their careers and those moving into positions of management who wish to refresh their skills. It is also of great value to graduate students of archives and records management, and to all information professionals studying for management.

**Principles and Practice in Records Management and Archives Series
Series editor Geoffrey Yeo**

February 2007; 256pp; hardback; 1-85604-584-6; £39.95